D0457215

AMAZING & EXTRAORDINARY FACTS

FOOTBALL

AMAZING & EXTRAORDINARY FACTS
FOOTBALL

ANTON RIPPON

David and Charles

CONTENTS

INTRODUCTION

Exactly where and when the first 'football' was kicked is a mystery shrouded in the mists of time. The origins of the sport, an offshoot of which would one day become a multi-billion pound part of the global entertainment industry, are too disparate and distant to pinpoint.

What is certain is that the form of the game we know today was spawned during the Industrial Revolution in Britain, when the working classes found themselves enduring long hours down the mines and in the dark satanic mills of England's North and Midlands, often in the most oppressive conditions. They had little leisure time to indulge in the hurly-burly of the old 'mob football' that had been enjoyed across fields and down streets in more bucolic times.

Ironically, the game's salvation lay with those who, hitherto, had had little to do with a rough, essentially plebeian game. Hunting, shooting and fishing were expensive pastimes for the sons of the new middle classes but it was they who, through public schools and universities, began to regulate and codify football. Suddenly a game of peasants and artisans required much greater discipline, teamwork and athleticism. By acquiring rules it assumed respectability. It seemed that the 'people's game' no longer belonged to the 'people'.

But when football clubs, born out of this process of codification and standardisation, realised that the more successful they were, the bigger attendances they attracted – and therefore the greater revenue at the gate – they began to look outside their immediate localities for better players, players who only through the promise of money could be tempted to move. Thus professional football – and the professional footballer to play it – was born, the 'people' took back their game and as a sport it has never looked back.

After the First World War (1914-1918) there was a significant shift in the game's position within society. During a series of economic depressions football was often the only bit of colour in an otherwise grey and cheerless world.

For thousands of unemployed men the prospect of a Saturday afternoon of escapism at a football ground held them together for the remainder of the week.

As J. B. Priestley put it in 1929's *The Good Companions*: '... not only had you escaped from the clanking machinery of this lesser life, from work, wages, dole, sick pay, insurance cards, nagging wives, ailing children, bad bosses... you had escaped with most of your mates, and your neighbours, and half the town... cheering together, thumping one another on the shoulders... having pushed your way through a turnstile into an altogether more splendid kind of life, hurtling with Conflict and yet passionate and beautiful in its Art.'

The 1920s and 1930s saw new football 'industries' springing up: boys' comics included pictures of star players, tobacco companies offered similar picture cards in cigarette packets, while an increase in gambling gave birth to the football pools. More and more money was being generated by professional soccer, although until well after the end of the Second World War (1939-1945) much of it did not remain within the game.

In the 21st century, however, thanks mainly to the tens of millions of pounds pumped into it by television companies – most notably Rupert Murdoch's Sky TV – football is a vastly rich industry in its own right. Many aspects of the game are unrecognisable from those of only a few years ago. Where star players once travelled to matches on the same public buses as the fans, and lived in the same terraced streets, now even the most modest professional footballer is likely to drive an expensive car and live in the 'stockbroker belt'. Players' salaries are now so large that it would take most supporters two years and more to earn even one week's wages of a top performer.

Yet still people flock to football, a game that continues to be both an amazing entertainment spectacle and extraordinarily accessible to people everywhere.

Ashbourne vs Ashbourne: late result
Who invented football?

No one knows who 'invented' football. Like the wheel, it must have been discovered in lots of different places. Just as no one person would have single-handedly realised that boiled eggs taste better than raw ones, surely no one group of people would have been alone in discovering the delights of kicking – or throwing – around a spherical object and eventually developing that into an organised game.

The earliest example was most likely *tsu chu* (or *zu qiu*, roughly equating to 'kick ball') which was played in China at least from around 2,000 BC and possibly as early as 5,000 BC. The ball was made from animal hair or fur stitched inside leather panels. The goal was a net measuring 12-15in (30-40cm) in diameter, strung approximately 30ft (9m) up between two bamboo poles. This was clearly a game for highly skilled players: they had to keep the ball off the ground but could not handle it.

Tsu chu eventually found its way to Japan where it inspired the game of *kemari*, a form of 'keepy-uppy' played on a pitch typically marked out by four trees – a cherry, maple, willow and pine.

Throughout history there have been all manner of other football variants, from *tlachtli*, played by the Aztecs with a ball made from rubber, to *epsikyros*, a cross between modern rugby and handball that was played in ancient Greece. Then the Romans took another Greek game, *harpaston*, named after a verb meaning to seize or snatch, and developed it into the faster, more physical *harpastum*, played between teams of between five and 12 players who could tackle a ball carrier by pushing him to the ground or dragging him down.

Royal Shrovetide Football sculpture of The Hug

And then there was the 'mob' football that gave medieval English peasants their recreation. This eventually took us to the organised game through the English public school system and into the universities, thereafter to be taken up by a wider public led by working men and spread around the world in various forms.

They still play mob football each Shrovetide in the Derbyshire town of Ashbourne, when the Up'ards and the Down'ards try to goal the ball on a 'pitch' – really the town itself – about three miles (5km) long. Sometimes they can play from 2pm until 10pm – without a single goal being scored.

'I'm going to play soccer'
The man who championed the amateur game

For England's match against Ireland at Everton on 2 March 1889 the Football Association selection committee gave an international debut to the gentleman who is reputed to have coined the word 'soccer'.

Charles Wreford-Brown

Charles Wreford-Brown was in his room at Oxford University when he was asked if he would be playing rugger that afternoon.

'No', he is said to have replied, 'I'm going to play soccer,' making a play on the first word of Association Football as the game was then generally known. Wreford-Brown, who also played first-class cricket for Oxford University and Gloucestershire, was one of the select few who could afford to play sport for no remuneration.

He was a leading figure in the famous amateur club, Corinthians, and a major influence in the formation of the Amateur Football Defence Foundation, designed to protect and preserve amateur football when it was felt that professional clubs were increasingly driving the Football Association itself.

The name was changed to the Amateur Football Association and, in 1907 when the FA required all associations to admit professional clubs, to the Amateur Football Alliance. Today, three current AFA clubs are former FA Cup winners: Old Etonians and Old Carthusians, who play in the Arthurian League, and Clapham Rovers. Past members of the AFA include Ipswich Town, Barnet, Cambridge City, the Casuals and the Corinthians.

Many of the AFA's affiliated leagues still maintain civil local rules that require clubs to provide post-match food and drink to opponents and match officials in a clubhouse or public house.

FIRST FA CUP GOAL
The FA Cup – the Football Association Challenge Cup to give it its full title – is football's oldest competition. Fifteen clubs entered in its first season of 1870-71: Barnes, Chequers, Civil Service, Clapham Rovers, Crystal Palace (not the current Football League club),
Donington School (Spalding), Great Marlow, Hampstead Heathens, Hitchin, Maidenhead, Queens Park (Glasgow), Reigate Priory, Royal Engineers, Upton Park and Wanderers. Jarvis Kenrick of Clapham Rovers became the first player to score an FA Cup goal, in a 3-0 victory over Upton Park on 11 November 1871. He also played cricket for Surrey.

'A fixity of fixtures'
The formation of the leagues

By the late 1880s football clubs and their followers were growing tired of the friendly matches that had to fill in gaps in the fixture lists when there was no FA Cup football scheduled. Friendlies lacked the competitive spice that laced matches like the FA Cup fifth-round tie between Aston Villa and Preston North End in January 1888, when a record crowd of 26,849 packed Villa's Perry Barr home.

During the game the crowd twice invaded the pitch, and to restore order police had to summon their own mounted branch as well as a troop of hussars stationed at a nearby army barracks. Eventually, midway through the second half, with Preston leading 3–1, the teams agreed that conditions were so farcical that the result should not count as a Cup match. There was no further score but the Football Association was having none of it: it booted Aston Villa out of the competition.

It might have been a disgrace but to one Villa committeeman it highlighted the huge difference in interest between Cup and friendly football. Villa director and 'father' of the Football League, William McGregor, wanted to see what he called 'a fixity of fixtures' where competitive football would be guaranteed every week.

In March 1888 he called a meeting at Anderton's Hotel on London's Fleet Street to discuss the formation of a league. At a subsequent meeting at the Royal Hotel, Manchester, the following month the Football League was formed. It has never been called the English League since McGregor always hoped that Scottish clubs would join it. On 8 September 1888

12 clubs from the Midlands and the North played the world's first set of league football fixtures.

INVINCIBLE PRESTON

In the first season of the Football League, Preston North End won the title without losing a match (18 wins and 4 draws). They also won the FA Cup that season without conceding a goal in the competition. No wonder they were called 'The Invincibles'. Only Arsenal, in 2003–04, have since won the top division of English football without losing a game.

Paid to play football? You must be joking...
Amateurism vs professionalism

On 20 July 1885 the Football Association finally accepted that footballers could be paid to play the game, although the move was inevitable. The continuous stream of Scottish players coming to play football in the north of England was down to one thing: money.

Yet the FA had chosen to ignore this fact. True, in 1882 it

had introduced a rule that allowed players to be paid legitimate expenses and 'lost time' from their day jobs. The following year, however, the FA suspended Accrington FC for openly paying its players. Bad feeling from northern clubs swept down to FA headquarters in London like a hurricane and it was left to a Lancashire club, Preston North End, to bring matters to a head.

Upton Park, a true-blue amateur club, protested that in January 1884 Preston had used professional players against them in an FA Cup tie. Preston didn't deny the charge. They admitted it, pointing out that professionalism was rife in the game and should be legalised.

J. C. Clegg, later as Sir Charles Clegg, President of the FA, was horrified. The legalisation of professional football would, he said,

'place more power in the hands of betting men and encourage gambling'.

In June 1884 the FA tightened its rule, forbidding clubs to pay any player more than one day's 'lost time' from work. It also banned anyone but an Englishman from playing in the FA Cup, a move obviously designed to threaten the livelihoods of professional players coming into the English game from Scotland.

The response was immediate: 26 Lancashire clubs, along with Sunderland and Aston Villa, proposed the formation of a breakaway 'British Football Association'. If that had come to pass, then English soccer would have seen the same sort of split that eventually created Rugby League from Rugby Union.

The FA bowed to the inevitable and from the 1885-86 season onwards, professional and amateur players played against each other, even in the same team.

Ironically, the Scottish FA still opposed professionalism and went so far as to ban from playing in any match under SFA jurisdiction 68 Scots who were registered professionals in England.

It was eight years before Scotland accepted that professional football was a tide that could not be turned back.

ENGLAND'S FIRST PROFESSIONAL

James Forrest of Blackburn Rovers is credited with being the first professional player to appear in an England shirt after the ban on professionalism was lifted. He received a match fee of £1 from the FA though since that was also the amount of his weekly wage from Blackburn, the club decided that it did not need to pay him that week. Forrest must have been happy enough because he later became a director of Rovers.

Penalty, ref!
Gentleman prefer to miss

$\mathbf{P}$enalty competitions. Love them or loathe them, today we are used to them. If the score is level after extra-time in a knockout competition, then we have the penalty shoot-out as it has come to be known.

That's not to mention the penalties, often highly contentious, that are awarded in normal time. Penalty-taker against goalkeeper, face to face, 11m (12yds) apart – it is always high drama.

Yet it took quite a while for penalty-kicks to be introduced into English football. The Irish FA suggested it in 1890 but the English relented only at the beginning of the 1891-92 season. They thought it ungentlemanly and, indeed, the famous amateur club, Corinthians, which was raised from the students of public schools and universities, used to miss penalties on purpose.

It was an incident in the Notts County–Stoke FA Cup quarter-final match on 14 February 1891 that changed English minds. With only seconds of the game remaining Stoke were denied an equaliser when the Notts left-back, Jack Hendry, handled the ball on the goal-line. The resulting free-kick was easily smothered and Notts County went on to reach that year's FA Cup Final.

The following season Stoke were again the victims in a match that saw another development of the penalty-kick law. On 21 November 1891 Stoke were losing 2-1 to Aston Villa when they were awarded a penalty with seconds remaining. Albert Hinchley, the Villa goalkeeper, kicked the ball out of the ground. By the time it had been returned the referee had blown for full-time. Later that season the law was changed to allow time to be added to allow penalty-kicks to be taken.

There have been many astonishing incidents surrounding penalty-kicks but one that was awarded in a Second Division match between Portsmouth and Notts County at Fratton Park on 22 September 1973 probably stands out as the most remarkable. Three different Notts County players – Kevin Randall, Don Masson and Brian Stubbs – all missed with the same penalty. The first was retaken because the goalkeeper moved; the second because the referee hadn't signalled; the third was a straightforward miss.

PENALTY EXTREMES

The first penalty-kick to be awarded in a Football League game went to Wolverhampton Wanderers at Molineux on 14 September 1891. Billy Heath scored to help Wolves to a 5-0 win over Accrington. On 22 October 2005 Arsenal's Thierry Henry and Robert Pires messed up a rarely seen two-man penalty-kick against Manchester City at Highbury. Pires was meant to tap the ball forward for Henry to shoot, but he mis-kicked and City defender Sylvain Distin was able to clear.

Kevin Randall

FIFTH TIME LUCKY

In the FA Cup first qualifying round match between Chichester City and Andover on 22 September 1956, a penalty-kick was taken four times before the referee was satisfied that the Andover goalkeeper had not moved beforehand. Finally, Chichester scored through their centre-forward Davis. But Andover won 3-2.

The cricket club that turned up by mistake
36-0 – and they think it's all an over

When Dundee Harp beat Aberdeen Rovers 35-0 in a Scottish FA Cup first round tie on 12 September 1885, they might reasonably have expected to have set a record. Amazingly, however, a mere 20 miles (32km) away Arbroath had just beaten Bon Accord by 36-0, still the highest score of any first-

class match ever played in Britain.

To be fair, Bon Accord shouldn't have been in the competition in the first place. They were actually a cricket club – Orion CC – and their invitation to compete should have gone to Orion Football Club. Undaunted, the cricketers turned up, called themselves Bon Accord to commemorate the password used by Robert the Bruce at the siege of Aberdeen Castle in 1308 during the Wars of Scottish Independence, and went on to make a little history of their own, losing by the maximum score possible in one over of cricket (if you assume no no-balls or wides).

Arbroath led 15-0 at half-time and scored another 21 goals in the second half. John Petrie scored 13 times, still the highest individual score in a first-class match in Britain. The *Scottish Athletic Journal* reported: 'The leather was landed between the posts 41 times, but five of the times were disallowed. Here and there, enthusiasts would be seen, scoring sheet and pencil in hand, taking note of the goals as one would score runs at a cricket match.'

Many observers felt that the score could have been over 40, had referee Dave Stormont not felt some sympathy for Bon Accord. He said later: 'My only regret was that I chalked off seven goals, for while they may have looked doubtful from an offside point of view, so quickly did the Maroons carry the ball from midfield, and so close and rapid was their passing, that it was very doubtful whether they could be offside.'

The possibility that their own score should have been even greater will have been of similar interest to Dundee Harp. The referee in that match lost count and thought that Harp might have scored 37, enough to take the record. But the Harp club secretary thought that his club's total was 35, and the lower score was sent off to the Scottish FA.

Two seasons later Arbroath hosted the real Orion FC in a Scottish Cup first round tie. This time the scoreline was a far more respectable 18-0 to the home side.

A game of three halves
*Electing to start again
soon backfired*

On 1 September 1894, Derby County arrived at Sunderland for their first match of the season, only to learn that the appointed referee, Fred Kirkham of Preston, had missed his train.

So the match started with a deputy official, John Conqueror, in charge and at half-time Sunderland were winning 3-0 when Mr Kirkham arrived at the ground. Derby were offered the choice of restarting the game from scratch which, not surprisingly, they elected to do.

But the next 'first' half also ended with the home side 3-0 ahead, and after playing a third 'half' with a gale in their faces, Derby conceded five more goals, making it 11 on the afternoon, only eight of which counted, of course.

Four months to complete a match
Roll on floodlights…

Sheffield Wednesday had every reason to be annoyed on Saturday, 26 November 1898. With only 11 minutes remaining of their First Division match against Aston Villa, the referee abandoned it because of bad light. There were, of course, no floodlights in those days.

At the time Wednesday were leading 3-1, but rather than let the score stand or, as was more usual, order the match to be restarted from scratch, the Football League decided that the teams should resume where they left off and play out the remaining minutes.

So, on Monday, 14 March 1889, almost four months after the abandonment, Aston Villa travelled back to Sheffield, where Wednesday added one more goal to make the final score 4-1.

One of the oddest things was that by the time the match had been resumed, both teams had to make changes to their original line-ups. Billy Garraty of Aston Villa, and Samuel Bosworth, Bob Ferrier, Ambrose Langley, Jack Pryce and Fred Richards (who scored the final goal) of Wednesday all played in only the final 11 minutes.

No goals please
Burnley and Stoke cheat the system

Having won the Second Division championship in 1898, Burnley were still not assured of promotion. In those days, the top two teams in that division had to play in a series of 'Test Matches' against the bottom two clubs from the First Division. A bit like today's play-offs, but with an almighty flaw: instead of a series of straightforward knockout affairs, positions would be decided on a mini-league basis. The system had worked fairly well to date, but this year would prove its undoing.

After each club – Burnley, Stoke, Newcastle United and Blackburn Rovers – had played three matches, Burnley and Stoke each had three points, Blackburn and Newcastle two each. Now Burnley and Stoke had to play each other – and if the match was drawn, then no matter what

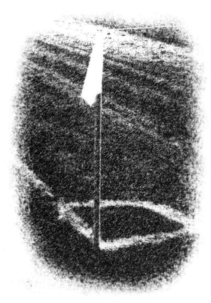

happened in the other game, both clubs would be playing First Division football in the 1898-99 season.

On 30 March 1898 a crowd of 4,000 braved heavy rain to see Burnley's visit to Stoke's Victoria Ground. They witnessed a fiasco. Neither goalkeeper touched the ball because if a forward found himself in a shooting position, then he aimed for the corner-flag. Eventually the final whistle blew with the score still 0-0. Burnley and Stoke had both achieved their objective.

The Football League immediately abandoned the Test Match system in favour of automatic promotion. When play-offs for clubs finishing out of the automatic promotion places were introduced for the 1986-87 season they were knockout competitions. Initially, they featured the club that had just avoided automatic relegation, and three that had just missed automatic promotion, but this was discontinued after 1987-88, since when only the four clubs that finished behind the clubs winning automatic promotion have been involved. There have, though, always been plenty of shots on goal.

Smallpox virus

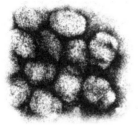

Poxy Boro stage a secret semi-final
Plenty of sea air the solution

In March 1898, Middlesbrough reached the semi-final of the FA Amateur Cup, only to find their way barred by a health scare. Middlesbrough had beaten Ledgate Park, Thornaby Utopians and Casuals before being drawn to face Thornaby FC at Darlington.

At that time there was a smallpox epidemic in the lower Teesside area and the people of Darlington, unsurprisingly concerned that the arrival of hundreds of football supporters might bring the infectious disease to their town, protested.

Initially, the Football Association sent a telegram to the Middlesbrough club, asking them to withdraw from the competition. After a hastily called meeting, Middlesbrough's directors refused the request. Instead, the FA agreed that the match could be staged in secret, behind locked gates at the Cleveland hill village of Brotton, two miles (3km) from the sea, where Middlesbrough duly won 2-1 to take their place in the Final, where they beat Uxbridge 2-0.

The only Romany to play for England?
Rabbi Howell's career overshadowed by controversy

So far as anyone knows, 'Rabbi' Howell is the only true Romany to play football for England. Born in a gypsy caravan at Wicobank, Sheffield, on 12 October 1869 and the son of a dealer in pots and pans, Howell began his career with local club Ecclesfield then moved to Rotherham Swifts before joining Sheffield United in March 1890.

Although only 5ft 5ins (1m 68cm) tall, Howell, a versatile player who appeared at centre-forward, centre-half, wing-half and full-back, had a reputation as a fearsome opponent.

His England debut came against Ireland at Derby in March 1895 and he won a second cap against Scotland at Villa Park in April 1899, after he had moved to Liverpool. With Sheffield United Howell had won a Football League Championship in 1897-98 but his final season at Bramall Lane was controversial. Often in hot water with the club for what it called 'off-the-field' activities that occasionally required United to top up his wages, Howell came under fire after a match at Sunderland on 5 March 1898.

Sheffield had lost 3-1 and Howell had a hand in two of the home side's goals, intercepting crosses that looked to be going wide and helping them into his own team's net. United's 22-stone (140kg) goalkeeper, Billy Foulke, made his feelings known about how someone of Howell's experience could commit such schoolboy blunders. The following month Howell was transferred to Liverpool. He ended his career with Preston North End and then, so the story goes, opened a fruit and veg business. He died in November 1937.

The enigmatic Nettie Honeyball
Just don't call her 'ornamental and useless'

In 1894, one Nettie Honeyball placed an advertisement in the *Daily Graphic* seeking those interested in forming a football club for women. She received 30 replies from women who wanted to play, together with another 20 from those who supported the idea. Thus, the British Ladies' Football Club was born, with a Tottenham Hotspur centre-half, J. W. Julian, as its coach and the feminist campaigner, Lady Florence Dixie, youngest daughter of the Marquess of Queensberry, as its president.

Honeyball was herself a feminist. In 1895 she told the *Daily Sketch*: 'I founded the association... with the fixed resolve of proving to the world that women are not the 'ornamental and useless' creatures men have pictured. I must confess, my convictions on all matters where the sexes are so widely divided are all on the side of emancipation, and I look forward to the time when ladies may sit in Parliament and have a voice in the direction of affairs, especially those which concern them most.'

With no other women's football club to play against, the British Ladies decided to split themselves into teams representing north and south London. The first match took place at the Nightingale Lane Ground, Crouch End, on 23 March 1895. There were 10,000 present although it should be said that a match between Crouch End and the 3rd Grenadier Guards had preceded it.

What did the lady footballers wear? Well, the Victorians were not ready for women in shirts and shorts. Voluminous blouses with knickerbockers or a divided skirt were the order of the day.

The north team won 7-1 and the reaction was mixed. The *Daily Sketch* told readers: 'The first few minutes were sufficient to show that football by women, if the British Ladies be taken as a criterion, is totally out of the question.' The *Manchester Guardian* reported: 'Their costumes came in for a good deal of attention... one or two added short skirts over their knickerbockers... When the novelty has worn off, I do not think women's football will attract the crowds.'

More supportively, *The Sportsman* commented: 'True, young men would run harder and kick more strongly, but, beyond this, I cannot believe that they would show any greater knowledge of the game or skill in its execution. I don't think the lady footballer is to be snuffed out by a number of leading articles written by old men out of sympathy both with football as a game and the aspirations of the young new women.'

British Ladies' Football Club

But the *British Medical Journal* was dead against it: 'We can in no way sanction the reckless exposure to violence, of organs which the common experience of women had led them in every way to protect.' It was ironic, then, that in April 1895 in Brighton the women played a match that attracted 5,000 spectators and raised money for local medical charities.

Other matches followed as the Ladies toured the length and breadth of the British Isles. Another crowd of 5,000 turned out to see the women play in Bury, where £100 was raised for local charities. More than 8,000 saw them play at Newcastle United's famous St James's Park.

Between March 1895 and September 1896, the British Ladies played 62 matches but towards the end only 400 spectators were bothering to turn up. Nettie Honeyball appears to have left the club in the spring of 1895, perhaps disillusioned by the fact that what had started out as an assault on the male sporting establishment had degenerated into a moneymaking venture hijacked by promoters. Nothing more was heard of her and she remains an intriguing figure. Her name is likely to have been a pseudonym.

Women's football's long march
From factory to football field

In the meantime, women's football foundered. In August 1902, the Football Association banned women playing against men. It was not until the wholly different circumstances of the First World War, when women were drafted into the nation's factories, that some formed works football teams.

Once such club, Dick, Kerr Ladies FC (Dick, Kerr & Co Ltd manufactured light railway equipment), was formed in 1917 to raise money for a military hospital. After the war Dick, Kerr Ladies travelled the country, playing to large crowds including one of 53,000 at Everton's Goodison Park, and even toured the USA. But in December 1921 the FA banned women's football being played at any of the grounds of its member clubs.

The ban was not lifted until 1971. The first official England team was formed a year later, and in 1993 the FA took over the running of women's football in England. Today, the women's game is an integral part of the sport worldwide.

First Ibrox Park disaster
'This football maddened crowd'

On 5 April 1902 Scottish football supporters were relishing the visit of an off-form England team to Glasgow. Many of them were also looking forward to their first close-up look at Rangers' Ibrox Stadium since its £20,000 revamp of two years earlier.

The ground improvements included two covered stands and spectacular inclined wooden terracing behind the goalmouths, each formed by planks bolted to a metal frame and housing 36,000 spectators. Alas, it was one of these terraces that was to be the setting for one of football's worst crowd disasters.

The game against England was the first international match to be played between two sides comprised entirely of professional footballers but it would not be remembered for that. Shortly after kick-off, on

Ibrox stands

the western terrace part of the huge crowd – according to some reports it numbered as many as 100,000, despite heavy rain – began to feel the ground trembling beneath their feet. Then rows of metal uprights supporting the wooden planks began to sway and buckle.

Finally, with a sickening crack, the terracing gave way and over 100 spectators dropped 40ft (12m) to the ground and were swallowed up by a hole some 50ft (15m) long and 13ft (4m) wide. The death toll was 25, the lives of many others saved by the fact that they had fallen on those less fortunate. Over 500 people were injured, some crushed in the panic caused by the collapse.

Yet after an 18-minute hold-up, the game was allowed to continue by officials who feared a much bigger disaster if it was abandoned. One newspaper reported: 'Nothing could better illustrate the vastness of this stadium than that 500 people should drop through a hole and the rest remain in ignorance.'

One witness was less tolerant: 'Not even the cries of dying sufferers nor the sight of broken limbs could attract this football maddened crowd from gazing upon their beloved sport.'

For what it mattered, the match ended in a 1-1 draw but did not count towards the Home International Championship. It was replayed at Villa Park, Birmingham, the following month. Again it was drawn.

The reasons for the Ibrox disaster were never fully established. Some experts blamed the quality of the wood but the supplier was later acquitted of culpable homicide. Rangers, meanwhile, removed the wooden terraces, reducing capacity of their stadium to 25,000. By 1910 that had again grown to 63,000 after new terraces used slopes made of earthen banks. Indeed, throughout football the disaster spelled the end for wooden terracing.

Chelsea and the Aberdeen Terrier
Canine ankle-biter creates a new club

One Sunday morning in the early months of 1905 Henry Augustus 'Gus' Mears, a well-known

London building contractor, was pondering what to do with Stamford Bridge Athletic Grounds and the large adjacent area of market garden that he and his brother, Joseph Mears, had purchased nine years earlier.

The Mears' ambition had always been to build a football stadium on the site, but they had never been able to raise sufficient capital for the venture. They were on the brink of accepting an attractive offer for the whole site from the Great Western Railway Company, when on that Sunday morning Gus Mears bumped into a financier named Fred Parker.

The two stood talking and Mears confided in Parker that he had decided to sell to the railway company as 'no-one will come in with me' to build the football ground. While Parker attempted to dissuade Mears from disposing of the old athletics ground, Mears' dog, an Aberdeen Terrier, bit him on the ankle, drawing blood. Instead of showing concern, Mears simply said: 'Scotch terrier – always bites before he speaks.' Before Parker could reply, Mears told him: 'You took that bite damned well, most men would have

kicked up hell about it. Look here, I'll stand on you; never mind the others. Go to the chemists and get that bite seen to, and then meet me here at nine tomorrow morning and we'll get busy.'

Within days, a meeting had been arranged with Archibald Leitch, a highly respected football ground architect. Eventually, the new Stamford Bridge stadium was offered to Fulham FC 'for their club matches only' but the parties could not agree the rent. Parker had a simple solution: 'If they won't come to terms, we'll start a new club.'

The first meeting of Chelsea FC took place at 7.30pm on 4 March 1905. By the following September Chelsea were playing their first Football League match at Stamford Bridge, all thanks to that little Aberdeen Terrier.

Heatwave at
Hyde Road
Manchester City's players
find it all too much

The year 1906 was a bad one for Manchester City. It began with their star player, Welsh international Billy Meredith, being suspended after allegedly offering an Aston Villa player £10 to let City win a vital game.

Then no fewer than 17 City players, together with the manager, Tom Maley, and several directors, were banned after it was found that the club had 'bought' the FA Cup in 1904 with irregular bonuses. And then there was the heatwave.

On the first day of the 1906–07 season – Saturday, 1 September – Manchester City entertained Woolwich Arsenal at Hyde Road. Because of the mass suspension of their players, City fielded virtually a new team. They also had a new manager, Harry Newbould. His City career was to start in the most astonishing of circumstances.

The temperature inside the stadium that day was 90° Fahrenheit (32° Celsius) in the shade, and one after another City's new men began to feel the heat. A crowd of 18,000 saw Arsenal take the lead in the 30th minute through Bob Kyle. Two minutes later, City's Irvine Thornley fell 'prostrate and very ill'. His match was over.

Tim Coleman made it 2-0 for Arsenal and then City lost Jimmy Conlin, despite his precaution of playing with a knotted handkerchief covering his head. When the teams took to the field for the second half, City's Bob Grieve was missing. Losing 2-0, down to eight players, and no substitutes allowed – there was nothing in the coaching manual to cover this dire situation.

Eventually, Conlin gamely returned and then George Dorsett scored for City. But soon Dorsett had to retire and City were back to eight players. Arsenal scored two more goals – one for Charlie Satterthwaite and a second for Kyle – before City went down to seven players when Tommy Kelso decided that he could not continue either. Finally, Jimmy Buchan disappeared, leaving the home team with only six men on the field. In later years the match would have been abandoned because a team needed at least seven players, but referee A. J. Barker of Hanley carried on. The gallant if wilting thin blue line held out, and the final score was 4–1. It could have been a lot worse.

Quite why it was Manchester City's players, and not Arsenal's, who had suffered so much from the heat has never been understood. Even then, City's misery was not over. Two days later they played at Everton and, although the weather had cooled and they finished with a full complement of players, they got hammered 9–1.

The election campaign scandal
Chairman wants seat in Parliament as well as director's box

On 17 December 1910 Middlesbrough beat Bradford City 3–2 at Ayresome Park to put themselves only one point from top place in the First Division. It had been a glorious season for Middlesbrough so far – 23 points from their first 16 matches. But then they managed to secure only nine points from their remaining 22 games. What had gone wrong?

Houses Of Parliament

It all went back to the visit of table-topping Sunderland on 3 December, when 28,000 fans packed into Middlesbrough's ground to see the only unbeaten side in the Football League. Two days later, another battle was to be fought, in that year's General Election. The Middlesbrough chairman, Colonel F. Gibson Poole, twice Tory mayor of the Teesside town, was standing against the incumbent Member of Parliament, Penry Williams, a Liberal.

Some of Middlesbrough's players had been on the hustings speaking in support of their chairman and, amazing as it may seem today, the result of a football match was becoming entangled with that of a parliamentary election. So much so, in fact, that Middlesbrough's secretary-manager, Andy Walker, approached the Sunderland captain, Charlie Thomson, with an offer: £10 for Thomson and £2 for each of his team-mates to let Middlesbrough win the game 'so as to help our chairman win the election'.

Thomson told the Sunderland trainer, Billy Williams, and when Williams reported the matter to the Sunderland chairman, Fred Taylor, the cat was well and truly out of the bag.

Despite a heroic effort from Sunderland, Middlesbrough still won the game 1-0. But irrespective of the result of the football match, Colonel Poole still lost the election – by 3,749 votes, a slightly increased majority for Penry Williams due to the fact that there was no Labour candidate.

On 16 January 1911, an FA commission suspended both Poole and Walker permanently. In a separate matter, Walker was suspended for four weeks for making an illegal approach to an Airdrieonians player and the Middlesbrough club was fined £1,000. At the club's annual meeting, shareholders were told that any further malpractice would probably see their club kicked out of the Football League.

All this surely cost Middlesbrough what would have been the only Football League championship in their history. The players never recovered from the claim that, for whatever reason, they had tried to bribe their way to victory.

Il Padre di Calcio Italiano
Unsung in his own country but a legend abroad

On 16 September 1911 William Garbutt's life changed forever. That afternoon he lined up at outside-right for Blackburn Rovers against Notts County in the First Division. Until the previous year, when Rovers had paid Falkirk a club record £1,800 for Jock Simpson, Garbutt had been a first-team regular. Now Simpson was injured and Garbutt saw an opportunity to regain a regular spot. Unfortunately it wasn't to be. He beat the Notts left-back once too often and became the recipient of a leg-jarring foul that ended his career.

He was only 29 years old. What to do next? Before the First World War many ex-professional footballers went off to run pubs. But William Garbutt had other ideas. He accepted the manager's job at Genoa.

Born in Cheshire in January 1883, Garbutt came from a large family. Desperate to escape the dreary conditions of early 20th-century working class life, he joined the Royal Artillery. Later Reading, then a Southern League club, spotted his potential as a footballer and he would go on to play for Woolwich Arsenal before joining Blackburn in 1908.

But now he was off to Italy with his pregnant wife, Anna, as the *Athletic News* of 26 August 1912 reported rather dismissively: 'Garbutt... has gone coaching at Genoa.' In fact, many of today's famous Italian football clubs had been founded by 19th-century British diplomats, clerks, factory workers and sailors. Genoa is no exception. Under the guidance of Dr James Richardson Spensley (director, referee, and goalkeeper of questionable ability) they won six Italian championships before their fortunes dipped dramatically after 1904. Yet Garbutt's arrival in 1912 heralded a revival in their performances, such that by the time he left in 1927 the club had won the Italian championship three further times. Garbutt went on to take the reins at several other emerging or top clubs in Italy including AS Roma and SSC Napoli before being booted out of Italy by Mussolini's Fascists.

'Unpatriotic and unproductive'?
Football stands accused of hindering the war effort

A fter war was declared in August 1914, the Football League and the FA Cup allowed the season to continue but soon the game was denounced as both unpatriotic and unproductive.

In November 1914, *The Times* newspaper carried a letter from the historian A. H. Pollard which said rather strongly that 'every club that employs a professional football player is bribing a much-needed recruit away from enlistment and every spectator who pays his gate money is contributing so much towards a German victory.'

The FA responded by claiming that 500,000 recruits had already been raised by football organisations; that, of 5,000 professionals, some 2,000 were already in the services, and only 600 unmarried professional footballers had yet failed to heed the call to enlist.

But the attacks continued. Frederick Charrington, heir to an East End brewery fortune, who had renounced his inheritance and found his way into the Temperance movement, was given permission by the FA to make a speech on wartime recruitment during the half-time interval of a match at Craven Cottage, Fulham.

For patriots like Charrington, who was seen by many people as one of those grim Victorian philanthropists for whom any entertainment was morally suspect, footballers and their supporters were moral cowards. Alas, no-one thought to inform the club that he had been given permission to air his views. As soon as he began to speak, two Fulham officials set upon him, dragged him down a gangway and threw him out of the ground. You've got to pick your fights carefully.

BOMBS AWAY!

During the early hours of 27 November 1916 two German Zeppelin airships, under attack from a Royal Flying Corps aeroplane, jettisoned their bombs over Hartlepool on their way back to the North Sea. Two bombs scored a direct hit on the town's Victoria Ground, destroying its wooden grandstand. For years afterwards Hartlepools United pressed the German government for £2,500 compensation but the only response they received came in December 1940 when more bombs narrowly missed the ground during an air-raid by the Luftwaffe.

Footballers come under the hammer
The great Leeds City auction

When directors of impoverished football clubs consider how to avoid things imploding around them, they might wish to consider the extraordinary example that saw one club's players auctioned in a unique sale of footballing flesh.

The Leeds City auction of October 1919 followed a scandal that brought a temporary end to League football in that city and must have sent shivers through boardrooms everywhere as officials waited to see who else might blow the whistle on corrupt football practices during the First World War.

It began so simply. When the Football League closed down in 1915, City's manager-secretary Herbert Chapman – a name later synonymous with Arsenal's first great era – went to work in a munitions factory.

His assistant, George Cripps, took over the administration while two directors, chairman Joe Connor, and J. C. Whitehurst, selected City's team for wartime matches.

Connor eventually accused Cripps of incompetence and replaced him with an accountant's clerk. Cripps moved over to take charge of the team and correspondence, but discord spread to the dressing-room when Leeds players threatened to strike if Cripps travelled with them to away games.

The Leeds board must have been relieved to see Chapman when he returned to Elland Road in 1918. Alas, their problems had only just begun. Cripps, now demoted to his former role of assistant, threatened to sue for wrongful dismissal. He claimed £400 compensation and added that he could prove that, during the war, City had paid wages illegally when the Football League had decreed that players could receive only expenses.

A compromise was reached: Cripps would receive £55 and in return would hand over all documents relating to the alleged illegal

payments. In January 1919 Connor and Whitehurst took possession of cheque books and letters. Sealed in a strongbox, they were placed in the club solicitor's vault. Cripps later claimed that he had handed over the documents in exchange for a £50 donation to Leeds Infirmary but had been refused a receipt to show where the money had gone.

Yet that still might have been the end of the matter, but for the intervention of Charlie Copeland, a Middlesbrough-born full-back who had joined Leeds in 1912. As City prepared for resumption of League football in 1919-20, Copeland's contract came up for renewal. Before the war he had received £3 a week with an extra £1 for first-team appearances. Now Leeds offered him £3 10s with more for first-team games, but no summer wages. This meant that effectively his income would be reduced.

Feeling snubbed, Copeland threatened to report Leeds for making illegal wartime payments. The board called his bluff and gave him a free transfer to Coventry City. Had they been aware that his solicitor was the same man who had also represented George Cripps, they might have had second thoughts.

In July 1919, Copeland carried out his threat, adding that he knew where there was a parcel of incriminating evidence to support his claim. On 26 September 1919, Leeds City appeared before a joint FA-League inquiry where they claimed they were unable to produce the documents. They were subsequently given until 6 October to change their minds.

When the deadline passed and there was still no sign of the documents, City's next game, at South Shields, was postponed. The inquiry met again and announced that Leeds City was to be disbanded. Although there was still no evidence of illegal payments, the club's refusal to co-operate had signed its death warrant.

Five club officials including Connor, Whiteman and, surprisingly, Herbert Chapman were banned for life. Successfully arguing that he had been absent from Elland Road during the period in question, Chapman was later reprieved.

Eight games into the season, Burslem Port Vale took over Leeds City's fixtures but the FA still had City's unemployed players on its hands. What to do with them? It decided to auction them and on 17 October 1919, at the Metropole Hotel, Leeds, representatives of 30 clubs cast their eyes over a varied collection of footballers, along with their shirts, shorts and boots – and even the club's goal-posts.

Twenty-two players fetched a total of £10,150, with high-scoring forward Billy McLeod the most expensive at £1,250 when sold to Notts County. Billy Kirton went to Aston Villa and ended the season with an FA Cup winner's medal. Billy Ashurst went to Lincoln City and George Stephenson to Aston Villa; both would later play for England.

Within hours of the auction, Leeds fans held a meeting in the city's Salem Hall and just a fortnight later, on 31 October, a new club, Leeds United, was elected to the Midland League to take over from Leeds City's reserves. The following season, ignoring a suggestion to amalgamate with impoverished Huddersfield Town, Leeds United was elected to the Football League. Leeds were back.

FACING THE MUSIC

There have been many reasons why professional footballers have left their clubs under a cloud. But one of the most intriguing must be that of Bristol Rovers full-back David Harvie, a fierce-tackling Scottish international who was nicknamed 'Hit-him Harvie' by Rovers fans. In six seasons with the Bristol club, Harvie made 238 senior appearances. But in 1920 he was ignominiously sacked after allegedly selling his landlady's piano without her permission.

All at sea
The Scottish club that found themselves foundering

When Raith Rovers finished third in the Scottish League First Division in 1921-22, it was a tremendous achievement. As usual, Celtic and Rangers took the top spots – that season it was Rangers' turn to be crowned champions – so the Kirkcaldy club could certainly consider themselves to be the best of the rest.

Raith's directors were so pleased that they decided to reward their players with a close-season tour – in those days a highly unusual venture for so small a club – and in June 1922, a party of 13 players and seven officials boarded the steamer *Highland*

Loch, bound for the Canary Islands.

The outward voyage was uneventful enough, until the night of the 30 June when the Raith party were jolted from their beds as the *Highland Loch* suddenly ran aground on some rocks off Corrubedo, on Spain's Atlantic coast. The lifeboats were launched and all passengers evacuated to shore.

The vessel itself limped into the port of Vigo, where it was found to have suffered extensive damage, including a huge hole in one of its bulkheads.

The experience did not seem to unduly trouble the Raith players, however. They continued with their trip, won all four matches, scored 14 goals and conceded only three. They could also now boast of being the only football club in the history of the game to have been shipwrecked.

SMOKE ME A KIPPER...
Football folklore has it that in 1922 Workington transferred a player called Forman to Hartlepools United for a fee of £10 and a box of kippers. Alas, there is no record of him ever playing in the Hartlepools

first team. However, when Derby County rewarded with a box of cigars the man who recommended Angus Morrison to them, they had certainly secured a bargain. Morrison scored 22 goals in 68 games before Derby sold him to Preston North End in November 1948, for the princely sum of £8,000.

A different kind of shot on target
Murdered by an angry neighbour

I magine the newspaper report: 'Aston Villa have been forced to make one change for their home First Division match against Liverpool on 17 November 1923: Vic Milne replaces the murdered 24-year-old Tommy Ball at centre-half.'

Signed by Villa from Newcastle United in January 1920, the powerfully built Tommy Ball had married the daughter of a local butcher in May 1922. They set up home in Brick Kiln Lane, Perry Barr, in a cottage rented from George Stagg, a former policeman who had been wounded in the First World War.

Tommy Ball

The men had a strained relationship – Stagg had threatened to poison Ball's chickens and had also tried to have him evicted – and on the evening of Sunday, 11 November 1923 their animosity boiled over into tragedy.

After an evening in the Church Tavern, Tommy Ball went into his back yard to fetch his dog. There he encountered his landlord; words were exchanged, a gun was fired, and the footballer staggered back to his cottage, where he collapsed and died shortly afterwards.

At Stafford Assizes in February 1924, George Stagg, who claimed that the gun had been fired accidentally when Ball attempted to wrestle it from him, was found guilty of wilful murder and sentenced to death with a recommendation for mercy.

Mr Justice Rowlatt still passed the death sentence but this was commuted to life imprisonment when Stagg was declared insane and committed to Broadmoor. He died in a Birmingham mental hospital in May 1966, aged 87. Tommy Ball, meanwhile, was left with an unenviable place in British history: the only professional British footballer to have been murdered.

One ground, one day, two matches – twice
Cuckoos in the nest

When Stockport County entertained Sheffield Wednesday at their Edgeley Park ground on 2 April 1921 there was something of a riot. Stockport were desperate for points in order to avoid relegation from the Second Division. At one point in the tense game, with Wednesday leading 1–0, the referee refused to award the home team a penalty. The crowd became so agitated that, after the game, windows in the match official's dressing-room were broken.

As a result the FA ordered that Stockport's final home game of the season – by then they were already doomed to relegation – would be played at nearby Old Trafford. Edgeley Park would remain locked and bolted.

And so it came to pass that on Saturday, 7 May 1921, Stockport met Leicester City at the home of Manchester United. That afternoon, United had hosted Derby County and around 10,000 spectators had seen the home team win 3-0. At 6.30pm, at the same ground, Stockport and Leicester drew 0-0 and the game entered Football League history as the one watched by the fewest people.

True, the official attendance was recorded as only 13 spectators but in fact as many as 2,000 people were present. Perhaps only 13 had paid to watch the second match but the rest had stayed on from the first game, catching the second for free. It was, however, the first time that a ground had staged two Football League matches on the same day. It wouldn't be the last.

Many years later, during the 1986 close season, Middlesbrough stood on the brink of disaster. Relegated to the Third Division with attendances regularly dipping below 5,000, they were heavily in debt. Only ten minutes of a Football League bankruptcy deadline remained when a consortium saved the day and

Ayresome Park

reformed the club as Middlesbrough Football and Athletic Company (1986). The club would be able to start the new season after all.

There was, however, still a major problem – Middlesbrough's Ayresome Park ground remained in the hands of the Official Receiver. So on the evening of Saturday, 23 August 1986, Middlesbrough (no longer on the football pools coupon) played Port Vale at the Victoria Ground, Hartlepool where, earlier that afternoon, Hartlepool United had drawn 1-1 with Cardiff City in the Fourth Division. The first match attracted 2,800 spectators, the second – a 2-2 draw – 3,690. Port Vale had complained about the venue but the Football League overruled their objection.

Strangely, having played their first 'home' match at the Victoria Ground, three days later Middlesbrough also played their first away match there when the draw for the Littlewoods Cup paired them with Hartlepool. This meant that Middlesbrough's first match back home at Ayresome Park would also be against Hartlepool, in the second leg of the tie. They duly repaid their neighbours' kindness by knocking them out of the competition, 3-1 on aggregate.

BILL'S BUSY WEEK

Bill Poyntz had an eventful few days in 1922. On Saturday 11 February, at Bury, Poyntz became the first Leeds United player to be sent off in a Football League match. The following week he got married in the morning and that very same afternoon scored a hat-trick in a 3-1 Second Division win over Leicester City.

It's raining goals
One-word change to the laws brings defensive chaos

Desperately searching for an antidote to the defensive sickness that stifled football after the First World War, the game's rulers came up with a simple remedy. But the results were astonishing. The cure did not just halt the decline – it revolutionised Britain's national sport.

Since the 1860s football's offside law had required at least three defenders to be between the last attacker and the goal at the moment the ball was played. As a consequence, full-backs could venture further forward. As long as the defence maintained a diagonal line, an opponent would be offside if he got behind the more advanced full-back.

By the 1920s, it was an offside trap honed to perfection by men like Newcastle United's Irish international defender Billy McCracken. More significantly, it threatened to kill the game as a spectator sport. Stoppages for offside had increased enormously. Football was becoming monotonous.

In 1925 the law was changed so that only two men were needed between the goal and the attacker to play him onside. The immediate result was a flood of goals as defenders failed spectacularly to come to terms with this new-found freedom for forwards. For a season at least, football anarchy ruled.

From the opening day of 1925–26, goals came thick and fast. By the following April, the Football League had seen a staggering increase in the total number scored. The First Division alone produced 1,703 – 511 up on the previous year – and, overall, 1,848 matches realised 6,373 goals, an increase of one-third on the season before. Huddersfield Town had scored 69 goals and conceded 28 when they won a second consecutive League championship in 1924-25; in completing a

hat-trick of titles, the Yorkshire club scored 92 but conceded 60.

As a result, the 1925-26 season was littered with some hefty scorelines: Aston Villa 10 Burnley 0; Birmingham 1 Burnley 7; Manchester City 8 Burnley 3; then, a week later, Sheffield United 8 Manchester City 3. Sheffield United, the First Division's top scorers with 102, beat Cardiff City 11-2, but then lost 7-4 at Bury. In one three-match spell, Bury beat Burnley 8-1, West Ham 4-1 and Manchester City 6-5. In the Third Division South, Plymouth Argyle beat Southend United 6-2 on the opening day of the season and went on to become the League's leading scorers with 107, helped by a 5-5 draw with Crystal Palace. In the Third Division North, Bradford PA, Rochdale and Chesterfield each topped a century of goals; Hartlepools United lost their opening game against Rochdale 6-0, but then beat Walsall 9-3.

Unsurprisingly, individual records also fell. Jimmy Cookson scored 44 for Chesterfield after being signed from Manchester City, who might have done better to keep him; they scored 89 goals but conceded 100 and

were relegated. With 43 goals apiece, Blackburn's Ted Harper and Bradford PA's Ken McDonald also set new milestones. It was a truly remarkable football season.

The crucial area of vulnerability lay in the centre. The centre-half was a major link between attack and defence – as the name implies, the central man in a trio of half-backs – and if full-backs pushed up as in days of old, a forward could now position himself between them so that he was still onside, and had only to beat one man before having the goalkeeper at his mercy.

Full-backs were faced with an almighty dilemma: if they played wide on the touchlines they left a huge gap in the middle; if they moved inside to narrow that gap, then wingers enjoyed yards of extra space to get down the flanks before swinging the ball over behind the defence. The middle had to be closed, and the man given eternal credit for doing that was Herbert Chapman who had just steered Huddersfield to those two consecutive League championships. Chapman's reign at Highbury had hardly begun when the Gunners suffered a humiliating 7–0 defeat at Newcastle. The day was 3 October 1925 and it was a disaster that convinced the new man at Arsenal that he must shore up the middle of the defence.

Chapman moved centre-half Joe Butler – like all his centre-half brothers, Butler had hitherto enjoyed a versatile, attacking role – deep into defence, and dropped inside-forward Andy Neill, a pastry cook by trade, back to link up in midfield.

Two days after their hammering at Newcastle, Arsenal won 4–0 at West Ham. Chapman's theory was vindicated. From narrowly avoiding relegation the previous season, the Gunners finished runners-up.

Arsenal's 'Chapman Era', with its FA Cup success and its own League championship hat-trick, was soon under way. By then, everyone had followed their lead. The attacking centre-half was dead; instead, the soccer 'policeman' – the man who stayed to block the middle – was born. All thanks to the changing of 'three' to 'two' in the offside law.

THE DAY GOALIES WOULD LIKE TO FORGET
The 1925 offside law change encouraged a regular flood of goals but on Saturday, 2 January 1932 a record was set for the most scored – 209 in 43 matches – in the Football League on a single day. On Saturday, 1 February 1936 the tally was equalled, although from one more match.

Dixie Dean – Goal Machine
The origins of the prolific scorer's nickname

Twenty-seven goals in only 30 appearances for Third Division North club Tranmere Rovers persuaded Everton to pay £3,000 to bring Dixie Dean across the Mersey in 1925. It was arguably the best signing they ever made: Dean repaid them with an extraordinary haul of goals – 377 in 431 League and Cup appearances.

The pinnacle of Dean's career arrived in 1927-28 when he scored 60 goals in only 39 League matches (for good measure he added another three in two FA Cup appearances). It was a remarkable feat, one that has never been bettered in English top-flight football. Dean also scored 18 times in 16 appearances for England, including goals in each of five successive internationals in 1927.

But why 'Dixie'? He was christened William Ralph Dean and neither he nor his family ever appreciated a nickname said to come from his dark complexion and a connotation of black slaves in the 'Dixieland' of the southern United States. Alternatively, there is a theory that it was a corruption of his childhood nickname of 'Digsy'. What isn't in dispute is his place at the head of the pantheon of English football's great goalscorers.

Dixie Dean

KEEPING IT IN THE FAMILY

When Birmingham City and West Bromwich Albion lined up for the FA Cup Final at Wembley on 25 April 1931 there was something of a family affair to the game – the goalkeepers were related. Harry Hibbs of Birmingham and Harold Pearson of West Brom were cousins who had grown up in the same Tamworth street. Albion won the game to complete a unique double of FA Cup and promotion to the First Division in the same season.

Ten-goal Joe Payne
It's always the quiet ones

Nobody saw Joe Payne as a goal threat. The Luton Town wing-half had been loaned out to non-League Biggleswade Town, managed only two Third Division South appearances for Luton in 1934-35, and four more at the start of the following season. It was all pretty unremarkable stuff.

Then came the visit of Bristol Rovers to Kenilworth Road on

Easter Monday, 13 April 1936. Luton Town had injury problems. In particular they had no recognised centre-forward fit enough to play. So they took a gamble and selected Joe Payne in that position, seven months after his previous League appearance, which was in midfield. And what did Payne do? He scored a hat-trick before half-time – and a further seven goals as Luton won 12-0.

It is still the only time that a player has reached double figures in a Football League match. After that game, Joe just couldn't stop scoring. The following season he scored a record 55 goals as the Hatters won the Third Division South championship.

In all he scored 83 times in 72 appearances for Luton and played once for England (scoring twice in an 8-0 win over Finland) before moving to Chelsea for £2,000 in 1938. For the Blues, Payne scored 21 goals in 36 appearances before the Second World War interrupted professional football.

After the war Payne had a short spell with West Ham United, scoring six goals in ten games before injury ended his career. A total of 110 goals in only 118 club matches left many wondering how many he would have scored if he had not lost six years to the war.

DEREK DOOLEY: FROM ECSTASY TO AGONY

Derek Dooley's early outings for Sheffield Wednesday were disappointing but when they recalled him in October 1951, he scored twice against Barnsley. And then he just kept scoring. By the end of that season he had notched up 47 goals, still a club record, as Wednesday won promotion to the First Division. But tragedy was to follow: in February 1953, in a collision with Preston North End goalkeeper George Thompson, Dooley broke a leg, and after gangrene set in doctors had to amputate the limb to save his life.

Stoley and the Argonauts' fruitless quest
Club that never played a game

The Argonauts Football Club was undoubtedly unique. Despite having never played a game, nor even named a squad of players, it attempted to join the Football League three times.

R. W. 'Dick' Stoley, an England amateur international who played for Cambridge University and Ealing FC, formed the club in 1928, naming it after the mythical band of men that accompanied Jason in his quest to find the Golden Fleece.

Stoley wanted it to be an English equivalent of Queen's Park, the all-amateur club that played in the Scottish League and used Hampden Park as its home ground. More than that, he wanted it to represent every amateur club and footballer in England and in that aim he had the support of the influential *Athletic News*. But Queen's Park was founded way back in 1867, was the oldest club in Scotland and one that had twice appeared in the FA Cup Final when clubs from north of the border were allowed to enter. It had pedigree.

Undaunted by a lack of football history or tradition, Stoley claimed to have secured the services of the

Clare College and the Kings College Chapel, Cambridge

top amateur players of the day, and to have arranged to play home matches at the 93,000–capacity White City Stadium that had been built for the 1908 London Olympics. After objections from local Third Division South clubs Brentford and Queen's Park Rangers, he switched the arrangement to the recently opened Empire Stadium, Wembley.

The Argonauts first applied for Football League membership in 1928 and finished 11 votes short of replacing Merthyr Town in the Third Division South. The following year, still never having played a game, they tried again, this time polling only six votes. At the third attempt, in 1930, the Argonauts received no votes. At that point, Stoley gave up the cause and the Argonauts faded from history, still having yet to kick a ball in anger.

WHAT'S IN A NAME?
The Football League player with the longest name is probably Arthur Griffith Stanley Sackville Redvers Trevor Boscawen Trevis, who played for West Bromwich Albion and Chester in the 1930s. Not surprisingly his team-mates settled for calling him 'Bos'. This could get confusing with the manager around, though.

'Back to square one'
Arsenal – in the vanguard of new media

These days football is everywhere: radio, television, the internet – sometimes it seems that life is just wall-to-wall soccer. But travel back to Arsenal Stadium, Highbury, on Saturday, 22 January 1927. Arsenal are playing Sheffield United in a First Division match, and history is about to be made.

Only three weeks after the British Broadcasting Corporation received its Royal Charter, the splendidly named Captain Henry Blythe Thornhill (Teddy) Wakelam became the world's first broadcast football commentator. It fell to Arsenal's Charlie Buchan to score the first goal ever broadcast on the wireless. The match ended 1-1 in front of a crowd of 16,831 who went home perhaps not quite realising the true significance of that day.

In fact, a week earlier, Wakelam – a former Harlequins RFC skipper – had delivered the first-ever running sports commentary on BBC radio when he covered the England–Wales rugby match at Twickenham.

As at Highbury, to give listeners a visual idea what it was they were hearing, a plan of the pitch, divided in numbered squares, was published in the *Radio Times*. As Wakelam described the play, a background voice mentioned the square in which the play was happening. Some claim that this gave birth to the phrase 'back to square one'.

A decade later, on 16 September 1937, an exhibition match between Arsenal's first team and the reserves was the first football match in the world to be televised live. Today, according to the club's website, Arsenal continues to be in the vanguard of new media with some four million followers on Twitter.

BBC *MATCH OF THE DAY*

Match of the Day *was first broadcast on 22 August 1964 when highlights of that afternoon's Liverpool–Arsenal match were shown on BBC2. The Anfield attendance was 47,620, the television audience an estimated 20,000. In 1965 the programme was moved to BBC1. The first colour transmission came on 15 November 1969, again from Anfield where Liverpool played West Ham United. With clubs fearing a drop in attendances, from 1965 until 1983 the BBC kept secret which match was to be shown until after the final whistle.*

The Football League's sabotage plan
But censoring fixture lists failed to drain the pools

John Jervis Barnard of Birmingham is generally recognised to have invented the first football pools, but it was three young men in a Liverpool back street in 1923, with a working capital of £150, who began what would become a multi-million pound pools organisation.

Barnard's 'football pool' saw punters bet on the outcome of football matches. The payouts to winners came from the 'pool' of money that was bet, less 10 per cent to cover costs. It was not particularly successful, and John Moores, Colin Askham and Bill Hughes, friends who had worked as Post Office messenger boys in Manchester, decided they could do much better.

First they needed a name for their enterprise. Colin Askham had been orphaned as a baby and been brought up by an aunt whose surname was Askham, but he had been born Colin Henry Littlewood. And so Littlewoods Pools was born. A small office in Church Street, Liverpool, was rented but the early venture never made a profit.

Eventually, Bill Hughes suggested they cut their losses. Colin Askham agreed. But John Moores was still convinced. He bought the others' shares, covering their £200 loss each, devised a security system to prevent cheating and the football pools that we know today took off. The Moores family did all the early hard work of checking and distributing tens of thousands of coupons. The main attraction of the pre-war pools were the 'penny points' and 'penny results', and five-figure dividends were not infrequent.

The influence of the pools became so great that it was claimed that they were responsible for the boom of interest in football in the 1930s. By 1936, the X-1-2 habit was a national pastime and the Football League, fearing that this form of gambling was detrimental to the game, decided to sabotage the football pools. Published fixtures lists were scrapped and games were rearranged and kept secret in an attempt to force the pools companies out of business since they would not be able to print their coupons in advance.

For three weeks the scheme worked and the pools companies were badly affected. But so was football in general: posters advertising 'Arsenal versus ?' were hardly going to lure in the fans.

Eventually, the fixtures were leaked by a 'mole' to the pools companies and the plan had to be scrapped. Instead, football's governing bodies decided to copyright their fixture lists and since then pools companies and other betting organisations have had to pay a fee for the right to use the weekly schedule of matches.

PEA-SOUPER SAM

The fog that descended on Stamford Bridge on Christmas Day 1937 was so dense that it caused the abandonment of the First Division match between Chelsea and Charlton Athletic. But nobody thought to tell Charlton goalkeeper Sam Bartram. For ten minutes he thought that play was going on up the other end and joined his team-mates in the dressing-room only after a search party was sent out to find him. 'I wondered why everything had gone quiet,' he said.

Thinking outside the box entirely
Football's unconventional managers

Time was when football was an uncomplicated affair. Even top players were paid little more than the average working wage – not three years' salary every week – and footballers' wives were more likely to be found down the Co-op than sauntering around Asprey's.

Football managers have changed, too. Nowadays, to manage in Europe's top leagues, they need something called a full UEFA Pro licence. Yet at one time football was happy to let loose, even at the highest level, men with only the slimmest credentials

for being in charge of a football team. Referees to part-time meteorologists – they've all had a go at football management.

When Sunderland were in their pomp before the Second World War, they managed to win the Football League championship and the FA Cup under the stewardship of a round little man who wore a bowler hat and was partial to a cigar and a whisky or three. His name was Johnny Cochrane and he'd once played for St Johnstone and had later overseen St Mirren's winning of the Scottish Cup.

According to the late Horatio Stratton 'Raich' Carter, who was Sunderland's skipper, when it came to team matters Cochrane tended to leave it to the players: 'Team talk? Johnny used to stick his head round the door at five to three and, in a cloud of cigar smoke, ask: "Who are we playing today, lads?" We'd chorus: "Arsenal, boss." And he'd just say: "Oh well, we'll beat them." Then he'd close the door and be gone.'

When Sunderland were on their way to the title in 1935-36, they suffered a succession of missed penalties but, again, Cochrane had

a way. Said Carter: 'We came in at half-time in one particular match where we'd missed another penalty, and Johnny started to tell us how to do our job. We knew he hadn't played much football, so one or two of the lads started ribbing him, asking how he would have taken the one we'd just missed. Johnny put his bowler hat on the dressing-room floor, we cleared a space, and he ran up and kicked the hat high into the air. We all cheered and mobbed him, telling him: "Great goal, boss." He just shrugged and said: "Well actually, I hit the bar."'

At least Johnny Cochrane had played the game. When Norwich City were struggling in the old Second Division in January 1939, they appointed Jimmy Jewell, who had refereed the 1938 FA Cup Final and had taken charge of the FA's 75th anniversary match between England and the Rest of Europe at Highbury. But he had never actually played football himself. Despite signing several new players, Jewell could not halt the Canaries' slide into the Third Division South. He left Carrow Road when war was declared and never managed again.

Another referee who went into management with a singular lack of success was Fred Kirkham, who officiated at the 1902 and 1903 FA Cup Finals as well as many international matches. In April 1907 he was appointed Tottenham's manager on a five-year contract worth £350 per annum. But he soon proved unpopular with players and supporters alike and in July 1908, his contract was paid up and he resigned. Despite his background as a referee, Kirkham showed scant regard for other match officials. In November 1907 the Football League censured him after he made improper remarks to the referee of Tottenham's match at Brighton the previous month.

Perhaps the most unlikely Football League manager, however, was another ex-referee, Captain Arthur Prince-Cox, former boy impressionist on the stage, Royal Flying Corps pilot and Fellow of the Royal Meteorological Society, who got the job as Bristol Rovers' manager in November 1930, despite only a brief playing career in local amateur football. He took up refereeing and reached the Football League list, as

well as officiating in 32 international matches throughout Europe.

Prince-Cox was appointed to the Bristol Rovers job from 200 applicants, no doubt impressing the directors when he turned up at Eastville smoking a cigar and driving a red open-topped sports car with white wheels. Prince-Cox survived for six years as Rovers' manager, taking them up the table without ever threatening promotion. It was his theatrical background that probably gave him his flair for publicity; he once chartered an aeroplane to fly amateur international centre-forward Vivian Gibbins from the London school where he worked to a midweek Third Division South match at Eastville.

When he resigned from football in 1936, Prince-Cox took up boxing refereeing and promotion and worked for the British Boxing Board of Control. He is probably the only Football League manager whose job it once was to deliver the weather forecast to Buckingham Palace. What would today's football rulers make of that?

Missionary adopts a principled position
Betting on yourself is not always a good idea

The African Cup of Nations was first staged in Khartoum in 1957, with three participating nations: Egypt, Sudan and Ethiopia. South Africa was disqualified when the apartheid regime refused to approve a multi-racial team. The competition now includes almost every African nation but football on that continent has often suffered problems.

In the late 1930s, a missionary in Northern Rhodesia complained that 'all the star teams play for money'. The same missionary witnessed a match in which the visitors bet on themselves and confidently spent their expected winnings in the local beer hall: 'Unfortunately they lost and the match ended in a free fight in which spectators joined.' In urban areas, football clubs combined with mutual aid societies, while migrant workers used football clubs to replace the material and social support they had left behind in their rural homes.

BROTHERLY LOVE – BUT NO CAP
When Harry McMenemy was named in the Scotland team to play Wales in October 1933, he looked forward to his first international cap. Unfortunately, injury ruled him out of the game and his brother, John, was called up to replace him. It turned out to be the only time that John McMenemy would play for his country. But at least he got the chance – poor Harry was never capped at all.

Passions run high at Hitler's Olympics
Peruvians pack their bags and head home in a huff

Although with a few exceptions it has been included in the Olympics since 1900, football has never enjoyed a particularly high profile at the Games. There have, however, been plenty of incidents, none more so than at the so-called Hitler's Olympics in Berlin in 1936.

In one of the early games, between Italy and the USA, a German referee, Herr Weingartner, sent off

Achille Piccini of Italy who then refused to leave the pitch. The fully professional Italian team had won the World Cup in 1934, leaving Olympic representation to the Italian universities team, themselves regular winners of the World Student Games soccer title.

The Italians, regarding themselves as giants of the game, were affronted by one of their players being dismissed against such an upstart soccer nation as the USA. Several Italians surrounded Weingartner, pinned his arms to his sides, and

covered his mouth with their hands. Remarkably, instead of a mass sending-off, the ref submitted and allowed Piccini to remain on the pitch and Italy won 1-0.

That, however, was nothing compared to what happened five days later when Austria and Peru met in the quarter-finals. Austria took a two-goal lead but Peru drew level with goals in the final 15 minutes of normal time. The game had progressed to the second period of 15 minutes' extra time when it too erupted into violence.

There are conflicting versions, but what is certain is that there was a pitch invasion. Peruvian supporters rushed on to the field and, according to the Austrians, attacked one of their players. The Peruvian players took advantage of the uproar that followed, scoring two goals in quick succession to win 4-2. Austria appealed and an all-European jury ordered the game to be replayed with no spectators present.

The entire Peruvian Olympic contingent promptly packed their suitcases and went home; in support of their South American colleagues, the Colombians followed suit.

In Lima, the German consulate was stoned and the Peruvian president, Óscar Benavides, was incandescent with rage over 'the crafty Berlin decision'. When it was pointed out that the world governing body, the Fédération Internationale de Football Association (FIFA), had made the ruling, not Germany, Benavides blamed the Communists instead.

'Heil Hitler!'
England told to salute the Nazi
bigwig but Aston Villa refuse

Frank Broome of Aston Villa had the unusual experience (for an Englishman) of being required to give the Nazi salute twice in as many days in May 1938.

The previous March, Germany had occupied Austria and no longer was there a separate Austrian international team – which had been one of the strongest on the continent – just one for 'Greater Germany'.

England were due to play Germany in Berlin, but the FA told the Germans that they could not include any Austrian internationals.

They agreed on the proviso that Aston Villa would play a German eleven the following day, and that team could include Austrians.

The FA's hope that Germany would not benefit from the Anschluss – the annexation of Austria – was realised. England won 6–3 in Berlin's Olympic Stadium, although one of the German goals was still scored by an Austrian, Hans Presser from Rapid Vienna.

The following day, Aston Villa beat a German Select XI 3–2 before 110,000 spectators who sweltered in 90° Fahrenheit (32° Celsius) at the Berlin Reichssportfeld. This German team contained no fewer than nine Austrian internationals. Broome scored in both games, only 24 hours apart.

During the pre-match anthems, the Villa players kept their arms tightly by their sides. England, on the other hand, had given the full-flung version of the Nazi salute after Sir Neville Henderson, the pro-appeasement British ambassador to Berlin, persuaded the FA secretary, Stanley Rous, and committee man, Charles Wreford-Brown, that

Air raid siren

there would be an international incident if they did not; and, anyway, Henderson pointed out, it was simply a courtesy to their hosts, not an endorsement of Hitler's regime. Perhaps most importantly, it would 'get the crowd in a good mood'.

The England captain, Eddie Hapgood, later wrote: 'The worst moment in my life, and one I would not willingly go through again, was giving the Nazi salute in Berlin.'

The penalties of war
When football waited for the all-clear

When war was declared in September 1939, unlike in 1914, the Football League closed down immediately.

Eventually it was agreed that some continuation of the game would be good for public morale and so regional football using guest players from among those stationed near to clubs was introduced.

There were many difficulties ahead before the League and FA Cup resumed in 1946, none more so than during the darkest days of the conflict.

At The Dell, a League South game between Southampton and Brighton was held up for 30 minutes after an air-raid warning. The attendance of just over 1,000 reflected people's caution at attending football matches when the Luftwaffe was likely to appear overhead at any time.

The following Saturday, with only 60 seconds remaining at The Valley and the visitors, Millwall, leading Charlton Athletic 4–2, the air-raid warning siren sounded.

The raid was a heavy one with shrapnel from nearby anti-aircraft guns falling on the stadium. The 1,500 spectators took cover and when the all-clear sounded, the game resumed and the final minute played out.

A week later, Charlton's match at Brentford was interrupted after 65 minutes. Again the players resumed the game, this time before the remnants of a crowd that had numbered only 600 at kick-off.

Playing football as the Battle of Britain raged overhead was a precarious and sometimes tiresome occupation. The Home Office had ruled that play must be stopped whenever the air-raid alert sounded. Clubs attempted to counter this with a system of 'spotters'; even after the alert sounded, play would continue until the spotter on the roof of the stadium signalled the actual presence of enemy aircraft. The government considered this too risky and refused its implementation, although eventually it was adopted.

In the meantime, matches continued to be interrupted, occasionally for up to an hour.

Players passed their time in various ways. Card games, singsongs, games of housey-housey, they all played their part in keeping footballers occupied while they waited for the all-clear. Some, however, got fed up and went home. When the referee went to round everyone up for a restart, often the teams could not be completed and so the game was abandoned. Not unnaturally, many supporters also decided not to waste their Saturday afternoons hanging around in air-raid shelters waiting for the football to resume.

In their different ways, most clubs suffered, not least when travelling to away matches. Reading's players had to stand all the way on a train journey to play Swansea Town. They arrived three-quarters of an hour late and lost 4-1. The following week, with a team that showed ten changes from their defeat at Swansea, Reading beat the Welsh club 4-0 at Elm Park. Whether the improvement in their fortunes was caused by the change of personnel or the short journey to their home ground was not recorded. Later in the season, Reading's manager, Joe Edelston, found himself pressed into service as a turnstile operator and unable to give his customary pre-match team talk.

Southend United, already deprived of their home ground because of the dangers of bombing, were dogged by trouble week after week. A match at Clapton Orient was interrupted after only eight minutes when the sirens wailed. The players returned after 75 minutes and began a match of 40 minutes each way, but just before the final whistle, another raid began and the game was abandoned.

Seven days later, Southend had to call off a game at Portsmouth because they could not raise a side. Then they had to play the first 30 minutes of their game at Norwich with only eight men. Sam Bell, Charlie Fuller and Frank Walton were delayed after the car in which they were travelling was involved in an accident. Southend lost 8-4.

Southampton's coach driver, returning from a game at Cardiff, became lost in the blackout, drove into a brick wall, and finally the vehicle suffered a burst tyre. The players were forced to spend the night in the coach, arriving back

in Southampton on the Sunday lunchtime. The players of Wycombe Wanderers had probably the worst experience. After a Great Western Combination game at Slough, the team had to walk the 15 miles (25km) back to High Wycombe.

DOUBLING UP

Wartime football was certainly different. On Christmas Day 1940 Len Shackleton and Tommy Lawton each played in two matches, each time for a different club. Shackleton appeared for Bradford (PA) in the morning and Bradford City in the afternoon while Lawton turned out for Everton (against Liverpool) in the morning and for Tranmere Rovers in the afternoon. On the same day Norwich City arrived at Brighton with only five players. Their team was completed with Norwich reserves and spectators. They lost 18-0.

BLADES STILL BLITZED 45 YEARS LATER

Sheffield United's Bramall Lane ground was badly damaged in December 1940 when the steel-making city was a target for German bombers. Due to wartime censorship, the **Sheffield Telegraph** *could not explain why the following week's match against Newcastle United was called off. In February 1985, however, local newspapers were free to report that a home match against Oldham Athletic had been postponed after an unexploded 2,200lb (1,000kg) bomb from that same 1940 air-raid had been uncovered close to the football ground. It took the 33rd Engineer Regiment (Explosive Ordnance Division) 36 hours to defuse it.*

Vic's Italian job
Living at the stadium with enemy POWs

S tepney-born Vic Barney was expecting to join Arsenal's junior ranks before war broke out in September 1939. Instead he was 'invited' to join the British Army, and although there were plenty of opportunities to play football – sometimes as many as four games a week – eventually he was posted abroad. Barney served in North Africa, Sicily and Italy before football re-entered his life in the most unusual circumstances. In 1945-46 he found himself playing in Italian league football.

Barney had been put in charge of the Vomero Stadium in Naples. The ground was in a dreadful state. The Germans had used it as a transit camp for prisoners before the citizens of Naples turned on their former allies in September 1943, fighting from street to street, door to door. After four days of German reprisals – troops were ordered to turn the city into 'mud and ashes' – the bodies of hundreds of dead civilians were dumped at the Vomero ground.

In 1945, with their own Ascarelli Stadium destroyed by the previous year's Allied bombing, the Napoli club arrived at the Vomero to start again. They found the pitch littered with spent bullets and scorched by petrol. With a staff of 20 German prisoners-of-war who lived at the ground with him, Barney was charged with the job of helping to make the stadium playable again. He did more than that: he turned out for Napoli who won the championship of a group of central and southern clubs. Napoli wanted him to sign-on when he left the army. 'It was an adventure. I still have the photograph of me, a lone Englishman, among a team of Italians. I shall never forget it,' he said.

After being demobbed, Barney played for Reading, Bristol City, Grimsby Town and Headington United (now Oxford United) before retiring at the age of 35. When he returned to Naples to celebrate his golden wedding in 1992 they remembered him. 'When I went back, the club president invited my wife and me to dinner. We were wined and dined before a game against Milan. It was nice that they remembered after all those years.' Vic Barney died in May 2006, aged 84.

What do you get if you cross a palm with silver?
The end of a barren run of 62 years, that's what

When Derby County reached the 1946 FA Cup Final, they had yet to win a major trophy since their formation in 1884. The reason, it was claimed, was that the Rams had been cursed by a band of gypsies who they had turned off land that was to become the club's Baseball Ground home in 1895.

The story didn't really make sense because the club got on well with the gypsies and one of them, 'Old Mallender', was even employed to mow the pitch.

Nonetheless, on the eve of the 1946 Final, an enterprising Fleet Street journalist took the Derby captain, Jack Nicholas, to a Romany camp in Sussex where a palm was crossed with silver, the 'curse' was duly lifted, and Derby went on to win the Cup.

Those mysterious Russkis
Incorruptible workers against corrupt capitalists?

In November 1945 the Dynamo Moscow football club made a short visit to Britain, ostensibly to further cement the relationship between two allies, but in reality to provide another reminder that Stalin's Russia would be a key player in post-war world affairs. The club came cloaked in mystery; they played shrouded in fog; and they returned home with victories on both the sporting and propaganda fronts. Their game was, in every sense of the expression, political football.

Football had been introduced to Tsarist Russia in 1887 when the Charnock brothers from Blackburn ran cotton mills outside Moscow. They formed a factory football team that, long after they had lost control, became a front for anti-Tsarist activities. In 1923 Felix Dzerzhinsky, the man who became founder of the Communist secret police, the NKVD, changed the club's name to Dynamo Moscow, affiliating it to the electrical

trades' union. After the Second World War Dynamo became the blueprint for secret police football clubs throughout the Eastern Bloc.

When they landed in Britain, Dynamo did so as the current Soviet champions. Both the NKVD and the Dynamo club had been inherited by Dzerzhinsky's successor, Lavrentiy Beria. In 1942, Beria had sent players from Dynamo's main rivals, Moscow Torpedo, to the gulag camps on trumped-up charges. This was no ordinary football club, popping over on a goodwill visit.

Dynamo trained at the White City before playing their first match, against Chelsea at Stamford Bridge, on 13 November. The official attendance was given as 79,496 but perhaps as many as 90,000 tried to watch the 3-3 draw.

When, a few days later, Dynamo beat Cardiff City 10-1 before a crowd of 31,000 at Ninian Park, the *Western Mail* commented: 'If British football is to compete with this spectacular stuff, we shall have to revise our views on tactics and training.'

On 21 November, Dynamo arrived at White Hart Lane for

the highlight of their visit, a match against Arsenal – Highbury still suffered from bomb damage – who fielded guest players Stanley Matthews and Stan Mortensen.

When London became enveloped in one of its famous 'pea-souper' fogs the match looked unlikely to take place. But 54,640 people had turned up wanting to see something of the exotic communists, however fleeting. At half-time Arsenal led 3-2 but the Russians levelled the scores and then went ahead. Arsenal had what looked like a perfectly good equaliser ruled out by the Russian referee, and at one stage Dynamo had 12 men on the pitch. They won 4-3.

Controversy also followed Dynamo to Glasgow, where they met Rangers. As in Cardiff there was a visit to see local workers, this time at a Clyde shipyard. The crowd numbered 90,000. At one stage Dynamo again had 12 men on the pitch, but after being two goals down Rangers managed to draw 2-2, thanks to a controversial penalty award.

After the four tour games had been watched by over a quarter of a million people, the FA attempted to arrange a fifth match, against a representative team at Villa Park. They selected the side, which was almost the full England XI, and printed 70,000 tickets. But the Dynamo party was called home before the game could be played. It was just another twist to a strange glimpse behind the Iron Curtain.

Dynamo's success in Britain was soon exploited by the Soviet regime. The players were made Heroes of the Soviet Union. A film of the trip was shown in cinemas across the country. This was picked up by Moscow's theatres and in 1947 a musical comedy entitled 19-9 (the goal tallies for and against) depicted the Dynamo team as incorruptible socialist heroes bravely battling against corrupt capitalists. By then football was being played against the new battleground of the Cold War.

Dynamo Stadium, Moscow

Thirteen goals – unlucky for some
Record score achieved three times

Thirteen goals is the highest number of goals ever scored in a Football League game – and it has been achieved not once, not twice, but three times.

On 6 January 1934 Stockport County beat Halifax Town 13-0 in a Third Division North fixture that proved to be a disastrous League debut for the Halifax goalkeeper, Stanley Milton.

On Boxing Day 1935, again in the Third Division North, Tranmere Rovers beat Oldham Athletic 13-4 at Prenton Park. Amazingly, only the previous day Oldham had beaten Tranmere 4-1 at Boundary Park. Seventeen goals is still a record aggregate score for a League match and the nine goals scored by Robert 'Bunny' Bell – he missed a penalty – that day was also an individual scoring record, albeit one that lasted for only a few months.

Finally, on 5 October 1946 Newcastle United beat Newport County 13-0 in a Second Division match before 52,137 spectators at St James's Park. It proved a perfect debut for Len Shackleton following his £13,000 move from Bradford Park Avenue. Shackleton scored six goals, including one hat-trick in only two and a half minutes.

Poor old Newport: after being promoted in 1939 they had to wait through six years of war before beginning again their first ever season in the Second Division. Their first match was then postponed because the pitch had become waterlogged; they then shipped 13 goals at Newcastle, and would endure a dreadful season before finishing bottom of the table.

Nonetheless, on the final day of the season Newport had their revenge on the Tynesiders, beating them 4-2 at Somerton Park to push Newcastle down into fifth place and deny them talent money.

Flying Doctor, Irish style
The double international who made sporting history

Within the space of one week in 1946, Dr Kevin O'Flanagan, an amateur outside-right with Arsenal, made sporting history by turning out for Ireland's rugby team against France before featuring for the Northern Ireland football team against Scotland.

Both games were unofficial internationals, but O'Flanagan was already Ireland's best-known international sportsman. Besides playing football for both Northern Ireland and the Republic of Ireland when players could represent both, and rugby union for Ireland, he was also Ireland's 60 yards, 100 yards and long jump champion and would surely have appeared in the Olympics but for the cancellation of both the 1940 and 1944 Games.

O'Flanagan made his international football debut as an 18-year-old in 1937, scoring in a World Cup qualifier against Norway. Altogether he won four official Irish football caps, including an appearance against England in 1948 when his brother Michael also featured in the Ireland team.

In 1947, he won an official rugby union cap against the touring Australians in Dublin. Michael O'Flanagan was capped later that season, against Scotland, making them the only brothers to win international caps in both codes. Kevin O'Flanagan, who later became an eminent figure in sports medicine and on the Olympic scene, died in May 2006, aged 85.

The Burnden Park disaster
Safety lessons go unheeded for decades

A ll roads leading to Burnden Park were packed on 9 March 1946. Bolton Wanderers were hosting Stoke City in the second leg of their FA Cup quarter-final tie, and the visitors had Stanley Matthews in their ranks.

Bolton held a two-goal advantage from the first leg. Would they prevail? Or would Matthews turn the tie Stoke's way? Over 85,000 people waited to see the outcome. But the ground's capacity was for just under 70,000 spectators.

When the gates opened at 1pm, tens of thousands of supporters moved forward to take up their positions on the terraces. Yet still the streets were choked as thousands more arrived. By 2.15pm – still 45 minutes to kick-off – there was hardly any room to move. Yet still the turnstiles clicked and clattered, feeding more people on to those terraces. Those at the front were pressed further forward, but it was now impossible for them to move in any direction.

There were no police radios; it was almost impossible for officers in the ground to communicate with those controlling the tens of thousands still hoping to gain admission. With ten minutes to kick-off, a spectator, trying to escape the ground with his young son, picked the padlock on an exit gate designed to spill large numbers back into the streets at the final whistle.

But people were not leaving Burnden Park; on the contrary, thousands more were pouring in. The pressure on the terraces was now unbearable.

At five minutes to three, a huge roar signalled the appearance of the teams and a sea of humanity swayed and rolled, desperate for a first glimpse of their heroes. Most fans were held in place by a series of strategically placed barriers that prevented the masses from pressing down to the front of the terracing. But there was one area, near the bottom of some steps, where no crush barriers had been erected.

Thousands of people were compressed into this gap, funnelling down uncontrollably. Then barriers elsewhere started to buckle under the strain, and down went the crowd, tumbling forward. Bodies began to pile up, two, three, four deep. Twelve minutes into the game, a police sergeant walked on to the pitch and spoke to the referee. Mr Dutton stopped play and took the teams off.

For 25 minutes the players sat in their dressing rooms. Word spread that two or three spectators had been killed. Then referee Dutton reappeared, telling the players that, on the advice of the chief constable, he was resuming the game.

When the teams took to the field again, they saw thousands of spectators were sitting over the original touchline, and new markings had been made with sawdust. The players were unaware that this was English football's worst tragedy to date: in fact 33 people had been killed, over 500 more injured. The game ended goalless, Bolton went through, Stoke went out. That night few people cared.

A Home Office inquiry found that there were no means of knowing when a maximum capacity was about to be reached, nor were there facilities for the immediate closing of the turnstiles. An attempt had been made to open exit doors, but the keys could not be found.

Several turnstiles had been rendered unusable, which meant that over 28,000 spectators destined for the Railway Embankment end had to enter from the Manchester Road, while ticket holders for the Burnden Paddock had also been admitted through turnstiles in this area and then escorted around the pitch to their places, adding to the huge build-up in the north-west corner.

In addition to the fans that had poured in when that panicking spectator had opened an exit gate, thousands more had simply climbed over turnstiles and walls. They had free rein: the police were reluctant to release any officers from the Burnden Stand where they were guarding food stockpiled by the Ministry of Supply.

A relief fund for the injured and the families of the dead realised £40,000, and a series of safety recommendations were made. Yet despite the huge amount of money pouring into football through the turnstiles in the post-war years, little of it was spent on ground improvements.

Forty-three years after the Bolton disaster, the Hillsborough tragedy at Sheffield in 1989 saw the death of 96 men, women and children, all crushed to death when too many people again found their way on to the football terraces. Only then was the lesson of Burnden Park fully absorbed.

Stanley Matthews statue, Hanley Town

The oldest player in the Football League
Emergency goalie sets record at the age of 51

When Neil McBain made his Football League debut for New Brighton in the first Football League season after the Second World War, he also made history.

New Brighton, members of the Third Division North, had appointed McBain, a former Scotland international centre-half, as their manager in July 1946 and he signed up virtually a whole new team for the return of peacetime football.

But on 15 March 1947 he found himself without a fit goalkeeper for a match at Hartlepools United. McBain decided that his best option was to draft himself into the team. Thus, at the age of 51 years and four months, he became the oldest player ever to appear in a Football League match. On a waterlogged pitch, Hartlepools won 3-0, but McBain was the real hero and afterwards the home club's directors insisted that he visit their boardroom to accept a stiff tot of whisky for his efforts.

McBain had made his first-class debut for Ayr United in 1915, which meant that his playing career had in fact spanned 32 years. In February 1948 he left New Brighton to take up the post of assistant manager of Leyton Orient.

Forced out of existence by sectarian violence
The tragedy of Belfast Celtic

From 1891 to 1949, there was no bigger football club in all of Ireland than Belfast Celtic, nor indeed one that provided such a focal point for the largely nationalist community it served.

The club's story is one of the game's most remarkable tales. Despite twice being forced to withdraw from competitive football, Celtic won the Irish League on 14 occasions, the Irish FA Cup eight times, the City Cup ten times and the Gold Cup seven times. The club supplied a constant flow of players into the Irish national team, and a steady trickle of footballers who were to enjoy good careers on the other side of the Irish Sea.

In 1912, when they were the first Irish club to play in Europe – they visited what, six years later, would become Czechoslovakia – their goalkeeper was Oscar Traynor, who would become a prominent figure in the struggle for Irish freedom and, eventually, defence minister in a Fianna Fáil government.

Between 1915 and 1917, Celtic dropped out of senior football for no reason that was ever made public. In 1920 they again left senior football, this time for a reason that was only too public: on St Patrick's Day that year, a semi-final replay of the Irish Cup between Celtic and Glentoran was abandoned when the crowd rioted and one spectator fired a revolver. Belfast Celtic closed down once more.

In 1924, the Irish FA persuaded the club back into senior football again. Their return marked the start of a glorious era with ten championships in 16 years. In January 1941, Peter O'Connor scored 11 of the 13 goals that Belfast Celtic put past Glenavon, an individual tally never equalled in a senior league game in the British Isles. In 1947-48, they went undefeated in all competitions for an entire season, winning 31 matches in a row.

Then came the events of 27 December 1948. Local derby matches are never more highly charged than when religion or nationalism is involved, and it was one such game, before 40,000 spectators at Windsor Park, that ignited the flame that would signal the end of Belfast Celtic.

By Christmas, the top two teams in the Irish League were Celtic and Linfield, a club supported mostly by people sympathetic to the Unionist cause. The match ended in a 1-1 draw, but that was academic. Each team had a man sent off, two Linfield players were carried off, and at the final whistle hundreds of fans invaded the pitch.

Irish News *offices, Belfast*

Celtic's centre-forward, Jimmy Jones, was thrown over a parapet, kicked unconscious and left with a broken leg, while goalkeeper Kevin McAlinden and defender Robin Lawler were also seriously hurt as the Royal Ulster Constabulary looked on, either unable, or unwilling, to intervene.

Even before the match there had been a lot of bad blood. Jones had been released by Linfield, but when he became a success at Celtic, his old club wanted him back. He alleged that the Linfield secretary, Joe Mackey, had tried to get him to leave 'those Taigs' and come back to his 'natural' home.

Jones gave the official short shrift, a response that unwittingly sowed the seeds of the Boxing Day riot. During the game, Linfield's Bob Bryson had been carried off with a leg injury following an innocuous looking tackle from Jones, but during half-time secretary Mackey commandeered the public address system and, according to Jones, 'was guilty of inciting the crowd by more or less laying the blame on me for Bryson's injury'.

It was hardly surprising that, when violence erupted, Jones found himself the main target for it.

That evening, Celtic's directors decided to withdraw from football at the end of the season. The Linfield club issued a statement condemning the thuggery. Dozens of their supporters also wrote to the nationalist *Irish News*, disassociating themselves from the violence.

Significantly, Celtic's statement heaped blame not on the Linfield club, but on the RUC officers at the ground. In April 1949, Belfast Celtic resigned from the Irish League, went on tour to the USA – where they beat the Scottish national team 2-0 – and then disbanded. Arguably, Irish football never recovered from its loss.

For the want of a boot
Remembering Indian football's barefoot generation

When India's footballers turned out in bare feet for the 1948 London Olympics, everybody flinched. Everybody except the Indians, that is. They were made of sterner stuff and went on to lose to

France in the first round at Ilford by only 2-1. And at that, India missed a penalty and France's winner came in the 89th minute.

One of the stars of Indian football, policeman T. Shanmugham, explained: 'We had a lot of inter-company matches between the British and local teams at the hard Police Grounds in Bangalore. The Brits used to play with boots, but we didn't.'

Then came the 1950 World Cup finals in Brazil. Bootless football had served the Indians well enough so far. Why change now? The fact that they had the easiest qualifying group of all time – their opponents withdrew so India didn't actually play a game – lulled them into the belief that all would be well in Brazil.

However, FIFA had a strict 'compulsory footwear' rule. When the Indian Football Association

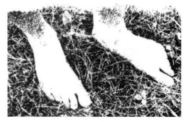

discovered this, they pulled out of the competition. Shanmugham recalled: 'I suppose we didn't know the rules. Perhaps that has always been the bane of Indian football.'

The goal that echoed around the world
The biggest shock in World Cup history – thanks to a Haitian immigrant

The newspaper sub-editor looked at the sheet of paper he had just ripped from the chattering teleprinter. And then he looked at it again. There had obviously been a misprint: 'England 0, USA 1'? England had obviously scored 10. Down South America way, someone's fingers had hit the wrong key.

But no correction came. And then further news filtered through to confirm one of the biggest shocks in the history of international football – England had been sensationally beaten by a team of no-hopers in the World Cup.

When England travelled to the Brazilian mining town of Belo Horizonte for their group match

against the USA in June 1950, they might have been wary. In their previous match, the Americans had taken an early lead against Spain and held it for more than an hour. Only in the last 10 minutes had the Spanish drawn level and then scored twice more.

England, meanwhile, had won their first-ever World Cup match, beating Chile 2-0 in Rio de Janeiro. Now, 300 (480km) miles to the north, they approached their second game with totally the wrong attitude. True, with players of the calibre of Tom Finney, Stan Mortensen and Billy Wright, they should have cantered home against a team of part-time footballers.

They did enough attacking to have won by a big score. It was only the acrobatics of the USA goalkeeper,

Stan Mortensen statue, Blackpool

Frank Borghi, and the efforts of the glove-wearing centre-half Charles Colombo that kept England at bay. And if you don't actually manage to score a goal...

The Americans, on the other hand, did score and their one goal was enough to provide the biggest shock in World Cup history. It came in the 37th minute, when Haitian Joe 'Larry' Gaetjens, one of three non-US-born players in the team, glanced the ball past Wolves' goalkeeper Bert Williams. For US football it was the finest hour to date. For England – the most humiliating yet.

Gaetjens went on to play for Racing Club de Paris before returning to his native Haiti. On 8 July 1964, the morning after dictator 'Papa Doc' Duvalier declared himself 'President for life', the rest of the Gaetjens family fled in fear of reprisal for the younger Gaetjens brothers' rebellious associations. But Joe stayed, thinking that Duvalier's regime would be uninterested in him since he was only a sports figure. That morning, the hero of the 1950 World Cup was arrested by Duvalier's notorious secret police, the Tonton Macoutes, and it

is presumed that he was killed some time that month. His body has never been found. In 1997, Haiti issued a postage stamp to commemorate the man who knocked out England.

POSH ATTENDANCE

On 19 November 1955 the first-round FA Cup match between Peterborough United, of the Midland League, and Ipswich Town, of the Third Division South, attracted a crowd of 20,843 to London Road, Peterborough. This was the first time that the highest attendance for that round of the Cup had been recorded at a non-Football League ground.

Injured goalkeeper locked out
Heroics in a 6-5 thriller

On 13 November 1948 Millwall were in the process of winning a Third Division South game at Walsall by 1-0 when their goalkeeper, Malcolm Finlayson, received a head injury and was subsequently taken to hospital.

Centre-forward Jimmy Constantine

The Hillary Street End of Fellows Park

replaced him in goal and ten-man Millwall – no substitutes allowed in those days – soon found themselves losing 3-1.

When Finlayson arrived back at the Fellows Park ground, having had his wound stitched, he found the gates had been locked. Unable to attract attention, the Millwall director who had accompanied the goalkeeper to hospital climbed over a gate and found a steward who let Finlayson back into the ground, where, 18 minutes into the second half, he resumed his place in goal.

This was obviously the signal for a Millwall fightback and they went 4-3 ahead before Walsall made it 4-4. Millwall scored again but again Walsall drew level. With just four minutes to go, Millwall's John Short scored again – it was his hat-trick goal in only his second appearance for the club – and Millwall emerged 6-5 victors, although not before Walsall had hit the crossbar. Millwall's win was the only away success in England outside the First Division that day.

GONE IN 20 SECONDS

Tottenham Hotspur wing-half Bill Nicholson made a sensational start to his international career, scoring after less than 20 seconds' play for England against Portugal at Everton's Goodison Park on 19 May 1951. But, thanks to the persistence of injuries and the good form of Wolves' Billy Wright, Nicholson was never again selected to play for his country.

In off the ref
Baily's goal should not have stood

On the Wednesday afternoon of 2 April 1952, struggling Huddersfield Town arrived at White Hart Lane, home of defending champions Tottenham Hotspur, desperate for both points in their battle against relegation from the First Division.

In the final minute, the bottom-of-the-table Yorkshire club looked to have at least earned one point from a dull, goalless draw, when Spurs were awarded a corner. The referee took up a position nearer the corner flag than

the goal and when Tottenham's Eddie Baily took the kick, the ball hit the official and knocked him over. Then it rebounded to Baily.

Under Law 17, Baily should not have played the ball again until it had been touched by another player (the referee is regarded as part of the pitch) but he crossed it straight back into the middle where team-mate Len Duquemin headed the winning goal.

There was uproar because the referee should have awarded Huddersfield an indirect free-kick, but after consulting with a linesman he allowed the goal to stand, a decision later confirmed by a Football League inquiry.

At first, the Huddersfield players refused to restart the game but there was no mass harassment of the match official. In their next

home match programme, Spurs commented: 'The referee's decision is final, and even if we have been the gainers in this instance there have been previous cases in which we have been the sufferers.'

That was no consolation to Huddersfield who, although they went on to be relegated by three points, might have argued that even one point that day could have spurred them to greater things.

FOOTBALLER – AND CIVIL RIGHTS ACTIVIST
Charlie Perkins, who in the 1950s had trials with both Liverpool and Everton before spending two seasons with Bishop Auckland, then one of the best-known amateur clubs in the world, later became famous in his native Australia as a fighter for the rights of Aboriginal people. He was the first Aborigine to become permanent head of a federal government department.

Deadly strikes of the lightning variety
Footballers killed playing the game they loved

On 19 April 1948, Royal Armoured Corps (Bovington) and 121 Training Regiment Royal Artillery met again at the Command Central Ground in Aldershot to resolve that season's Army Cup Final. However even 30 minutes' extra time had failed to produce a goal in the first game.

Inside 20 minutes of the replay, with thunder rumbling in the distance, the Artillery team scored twice. Then there was a lightning flash directly over the pitch. All the players, including future England Test cricketer Jack Flavell and the referee, fell to the ground. It was a minute or two before they began to stagger to their feet... all except for two players, one from either team. They lay completely motionless, killed. Three other players and the referee, as well as two spectators, were seriously injured. The match was abandoned and the trophy was shared.

That wasn't to be the only time a footballer was killed by lighting. On 25 February 1967 heavy rain fell as Highgate United and Enfield kicked-off their FA Amateur Cup quarter-final tie at the Tythe Barn Lane ground, just outside Solihull in the West Midlands, where temporary stands had been added to accommodate a larger than average crowd of around 2,000.

The match had been going for about half an hour when the

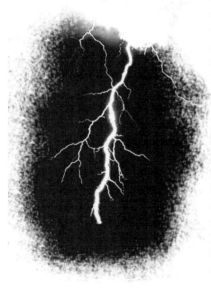

Highgate United centre-half, Tony Allden, was struck by lightning. The match was abandoned and Allden was taken to Solihull Hospital where the following day he died from his injuries. When the game was replayed, ten days later at Villa Park, a crowd of over 30,000 turned out to pay tribute to an amateur footballer of whom they had never heard until that dreadful day.

In October 1998, in the strife-ridden central African state of the Democratic Republic of Congo, there were accusations of witchcraft when lightning struck dead an entire football team on the pitch in the eastern province of Kasai – but left their opponents completely unharmed.

The Kinshasa daily newspaper *L'Avenir* reported: 'Lightning killed at a stroke 11 young people aged between 20 and 35 years during a football match... The athletes from Basanga [the home team] curiously came out of this catastrophe unscathed... The exact nature of the lightning has divided the population in this region which is known for its use of fetishes in football.'

DROWNED WHILE SEARCHING FOR BALL

In December 2006 Alessio Ferramosca and Riccardo Neri, members of the Juventus youth team, drowned in an artificial lake inside the Italian club's sports centre after falling in the ice-cold water as they tried to retrieve a football.

The cruellest way to be KO'd in the Cup?
Blindfolded Roman boy controls football fates

Those who think that penalty shoot-outs and 'golden goals' are a cruel way to decide a football cup-tie might think again after considering what happened in Rome in March 1954.

When Spain learned that they had been drawn in the same group as Turkey in the qualifying competition for that year's World Cup, they felt pleased. Especially since there was no one else involved thanks to FIFA's eccentric decision to split the qualifiers into 13 sections, four comprising only two teams each.

After the first match, in Madrid on 6 January 1954, Spanish hopes soared even higher. A crowd of 110,000 had seen the home side win 4-0 against one of the tournament's rank outsiders. But a week later, in the Mithat Pasha Stadium in Istanbul, the Turks took the lead after ten minutes and held on for a famous victory.

Of course, had the aggregate score counted, then the Spaniards would have gone through to the finals in Switzerland later that year. But the rules decreed that there should be a play-off on neutral ground.

Thus, on 17 March the teams met again in Rome, where a remarkably large crowd of 60,000 mostly neutral fans watched the teams fight out a 2-2 draw.

What to do next? Well, the football was over. There was no provision for another game, or even for 30 minutes' extra time. The stalemate was to be resolved by drawing lots. A 14-year-old Roman named Luigi Franco Gemma, son of a stadium employee, was blindfolded and asked to draw one name from a pot.

Athletico Madrid's Adrian Escudero, scorer of Spain's second goal in Rome, later recalled: 'We shut ourselves away in the dressing-room feeling utterly dispirited, thinking that there was nothing more we could do, that everything had gone so badly that the kid wouldn't pick our name. And of course, he didn't. The disappointment was tremendous.'

So Turkey went through, but there was some poetic justice when in their finals group the Turks finished level on points with third-placed West Germany but with a better goal difference. FIFA ordered a play-off in Zurich. The Germans won 7-2.

Turkey went home. Spain simply reflected on what might have been.

THE LIGHTS ARE ON BUT IS ANYONE AT HOME?
England played their first full international match under floodlights in a baseball stadium. On June 1953, they beat the USA 6–3 at Yankee Stadium, New York. The match, which had been postponed for 24 hours because of heavy rain, attracted an attendance of only 10,000 curious American sports fans.

Yankee Stadium, New York

Six old boys hit six
Rejects return to shock former club

The *News Chronicle* had summed it up: 'Of all the tiny clubs fighting for Cup glory this weekend, none has a dimmer chance than Boston.'

So when the football results began to splutter into newspaper offices across Britain on a murky Saturday afternoon in December 1955, sub-editors blinked in astonishment at one particular scoreline: Derby County 1 Boston United 6.

It did not end there. The Boston team contained six former Derby players. Throughout the colourful history of the FA Cup, with all its giant-killing feats and all its glorious romance, there had never been a result quite like this.

That season's second-round draw had thrown up one of those coincidences for which the competition is famous. Non-League minnows Boston, whose player-manager was former Derby goalkeeper Ray Middleton, also included Reg Harrison, an FA Cup winner with Derby in 1946, and

four more ex-Derby players who had played mostly in the reserves.

Even allowing for the fact that Derby had just been relegated to the Third Division North for the first time in their history, there was little to suggest that they would not triumph. But it was Boston – with derisive chants of 'Derby old boys' ringing in their ears – who took command from the start. After 26 minutes they went in front through former Derby player Ray Wilkins.

The majority of the 23,767 crowd were surprised but not unduly worried. Seven minutes later they were beginning to panic when another ex-Derby reserve Geoff Hazledine made it 2-0. Although Derby's former Wolves and England inside-forward Jesse Pye scored from the penalty spot, Boston were soon back on the attack and before half-time had restored their two-goal lead when Johnny Birbeck rose to head home the Lincolnshire club's third.

Derby emerged for the second half without the injured defender Martin McDonnell, and their ten men were no match for a rampant Boston. Geoff Hazledine linked up with Wilkins for two carbon-copy goals to complete his hat-trick. And 12 minutes from time, Wilkins took a pass from Harrison to complete an astonishing rout.

Don't bother asking survivors of the Derby side to tell you about the day their rejected team-mates returned to humiliate them. It may be nearly 60 years ago, but still none of them will talk about it.

A LINESMAN BY ANY OTHER NAME

When Leyton Orient met Newport County in a Third Division South match at Brisbane Road on 27 September 1952, one of the linesmen was named 'A. Newport'. He did his namesakes no favours, however; the visitors lost 2-1.

Cycling in the dark
How England stars used to fall foul of the law

Perhaps nothing provides a starker contrast between the lives of present-day professional footballers and those of yesteryear than their mode of transport. Today, players drive top-of-the-range sports cars or 4x4s. In days gone by, they used the same public transport as the fans. Or they got on their bikes.

Occasionally, footballers find themselves in trouble with the law over their choice of transport. Again, though, the contrast could not be greater. Take the cases of two Manchester United players, 55 years apart.

In January 2010, United star Darren Fletcher was ordered to pay more than £1,500 after Penrith Magistrates' Court heard how Fletcher's father had been caught speeding while driving the footballer's 2007-reg Range Rover on the M6 in Cumbria in November 2008.

Fletcher had not responded to a request from Cumbria Police and was charged with 'failing to give information re driver's identity'. After a half-day trial the Scotland international player was given six penalty points, fined £625 and ordered to pay £900 prosecution costs and £15 victim surcharge.

Contrast this with the case of Duncan Edwards of Manchester United and England, who was regarded as the football superstar of his generation before his tragic death at Munich in 1958. After playing in a local derby against Manchester City at Old Trafford on 12 February 1955,

Edwards was caught by the police riding home on his bike without lights. He was fined five shillings (25p) by the court, while Manchester United docked him two weeks' wages for bringing their name into disrepute. It added insult to injury for Edwards whose team had been beaten 5-0 that day. How times change...

The child star whose career was on hold for seven years
Manchester United wanted him – before he broke his leg

When Alick Jeffrey played for Doncaster Rovers in an FA Cup tie at Villa Park on 29 January 1955 it was a wonderful way to celebrate his 16th birthday.

In fact Jeffrey had made his debut for Doncaster when he was only 15 years old and had already caught the attention of Manchester United. Then tragedy struck.

The hugely talented youngster had scored 34 goals in only 71 games for Doncaster when in October 1956 he broke his right leg playing for the England Under-23s. He was forced to

Duncan Edwards statue, Dudley

at 104mph (165kph) in a 50mph (80kph) zone in his £150,000 Lamborghini Gallardo. At the time Cole was reported to be earning £100,000 a week. He later claimed he was trying to escape paparazzi.

The greatest comeback?
5-1 down and yet they still win

After 17 minutes of their Second Division match against Huddersfield Town at The Valley on 21 December 1957, things looked bleak for Charlton Athletic. Down to ten men, they were losing 2-0. And it was about to get even worse.

Charlton had lost centre-half Derek Ufton with a dislocated shoulder and were behind to goals from Huddersfield's Les Massie and Alex Bain. And although Johnny Summers made it 2-1 two minutes into the second half, another goal from Bain and one each from Bill McGarry, from the penalty spot, and Bob Ledger made it 5-1 to the visitors with less than half an hour to play.

Many in the 12,535 crowd decided to leave. They missed a Christmas

retire but fought back and, after seven years out of League football, rejoined Doncaster, going on to score another 95 goals in 191 appearances for them.

'CASHLEY' COLE – NEEDS TIME TO PAY
When Chelsea and England defender Ashley Cole was fined £1,000 and banned from driving for four months in January 2010 his solicitor caused pained smiles at Kingston magistrates court by asking if the player could have 21 days to pay. His misdemeanour? He had been driving

football miracle. Within two minutes of Huddersfield's fifth goal, Charlton had pegged the score back to 5-3 with goals from Buck Ryan and Summers. Then, in an amazing eight minutes, Summers scored three more to put Charlton 6-5 in front.

Yet still it wasn't over. With four minutes remaining, Stan Howard equalised for Huddersfield before Ryan hit the winner for the home side deep into stoppage time with only seconds to play. It remains the only time that a 7-6 scoreline has been recorded in the Football League.

As it happened, in that era Charlton were no strangers to goal-rush scorelines. On 22 October 1960 they drew 6-6 with Middlesbrough at The Valley. Three weeks earlier, Summers had scored five goals in a 7-4 home victory over Portsmouth. In November 1959 Charlton were beaten 11-1 at Aston Villa and, six weeks before that, had lost 6-4 at Plymouth. Amazingly, the following season Charlton had two more 6-4 results against Plymouth, winning the home match on Boxing Day 1960 but losing the return match played just 24 hours later.

Just to add to the coincidences, Derek Ufton had been injured against Huddersfield in the opening match of the 1957-58 season, although on that occasion it was the Yorkshire club that staged a remarkable recovery when they fought back from 3-0 down to draw 3-3. Ufton had also dislocated a shoulder against Huddersfield at The Valley in November 1953. On that occasion, Charlton won 2-1 after trailing a goal down.

UNDERSOIL HEATING WORKED TOO WELL
In May 1958 Everton became the first Football League club to install undersoil heating when some 20 miles (32km) of electric wire was buried beneath the Goodison Park pitch at a cost of £16,000. It worked. In fact, as things turned out, it

worked rather too well. The system melted frost and ice most effectively, but the drains could not handle the extra quantities of water. In 1960 the pitch had to be dug up again for new drainage pipes to be laid.

'Is he the type to captain England?'
The corridors of moral power

When Billy Wright played his last game for England, against the USA in Los Angeles on 28 May 1959, it marked the end of a world record run of 70 consecutive international appearances that began against France on 3 October 1951.

And when Wright had made his final appearance against Scotland, on 11 April 1959, it marked a record 25 consecutive appearances in the Home International Championship. Wright also captained his country a record 90 times in 105 appearances.

However, he was not always a favourite with the Football Association's international selection committee. During the 1958 World Cup finals in Sweden even squeaky-clean Wright's reputation was called into question when it was announced that he was to marry one of the Beverley Sisters (biggest hit: 'I Saw Mommy Kissing Santa Claus'). The problem was that the lady in question, Joy Beverley, was a divorcée.

We're hardly talking a John Terry–Vanessa Perroncel sex scandal

Billy Wright statue, Wolverhampton

here, but this was still enough to send the frowning blazer-wearers in the FA committee room spinning into a state of near apoplexy.

'Is this the sort of man we want captaining England?' they asked each other. Eventually, because Wright's playing career was nearing its end, they decided to forget about it, and one of English football's greatest servants was allowed to retire gracefully.

WAGE-CAPPING

Consider the tens of thousands of pounds in wages that top footballers earn each week in the 21st century and compare it to the maximum wage scale in 1956: full-time player at age 17, playing season £7, close season £6; at age of 18, £9 and £8; 19 years of age, £11.10s and £10; at age of 20 and over, £15 and £12. Match bonuses of £2 for a win and £1 for a draw were allowed for 11 players and one reserve.

Lincoln City's mighty reprieve
The Imps win six in a row to avoid relegation

With only six matches remaining of their 1957-58 season Lincoln City looked doomed to relegation from the Second Division. They had won only five of their 36 League matches and had not scented victory for four months.

Their remaining fixtures – three home matches, three away – were not against the leading clubs, but when you are rock-bottom of the table every game is daunting, especially when some of your opponents are also in trouble and desperate for points.

Yet Lincoln won every one of those final six matches to avoid relegation by only one point. It was certainly a great escape. How did they manage it?

They began with a 3-1 win at Barnsley, then beat second-from-bottom Doncaster Rovers 3-1, and triumphed 2-0 against Rotherham United and 4-0 over Bristol City. An away game at Huddersfield Town

Lincoln City fans

looked a difficult proposition, but Lincoln won 1-0 and came away with both points.

That just left Cardiff City. Over 18,000 fans crammed into Lincoln's Sincil Bank ground on 30 April 1958. They saw Cardiff take an early lead. Everything that had recently gone before appeared to count for nothing. With only 20 minutes remaining, Lincoln were still losing. But then they scored three times in ten minutes. Against all the odds, they were safe. It was remarkable.

In fact, it was extraordinary. Lincoln

had already met Cardiff at Lincoln that season and had been losing 3-0 when a blizzard saved them by forcing the match to be postponed. Talk about second chances.

NOTHING TO SMILE ABOUT
In April 1960 referee Henning Erikstrup was about to signal the end of a Danish match between Nørager and Ebeltoft when his false teeth fell out. While Mr Erikstrup scrambled to retrieve his dentures, Ebeltoft went away to score what they thought was

an equalising goal. But the referee, now with a full set again, disallowed their effort and blew the final whistle.

Double hat-tricks – not good enough
The highest scoring losers in FA Cup history

You might think that if you scored six goals in one FA Cup match, then your team would progress to the next round. Yet when Denis Law scored six times for Manchester City against Luton Town in a fourth-round match at Kenilworth Road on 28 January 1961, he still finished on the losing side.

Thanks to Law's double hat-trick, City were winning 6-2 when the pitch became so waterlogged that the referee abandoned the match. When the teams started from scratch on 1 February, Law again scored for City. But it was Luton who emerged victorious, 3-1.

Had Law's goals from the original match counted, he would have topped the 20th-century's list of FA Cup scorers. Instead, that honour

went to Ian Rush with 44 FA Cup goals (Liverpool 39, Chester 4 and Newcastle United 1). Law finished second with 41 (Manchester United 34, Manchester City 4 and Huddersfield Town 3).

Denis Law, however, isn't the highest losing scorer in FA Cup history. In November 1922 Wilfred Minter scored all seven of Athenian League champions St Albans City's goals in a fourth qualifying round

The United Trinity *statue of Charlton (right) alongside Denis Law (centre) and George Best (left), Old Trafford*

replay at Dulwich Hamlet of the Isthmian League. Unfortunately for Minter, his side, fielding a stand-in goalkeeper, conceded eight. Minter, an England amateur international, scored 356 goals in 362 matches for St Albans but refused all offers to turn professional in favour of working in the family business.

CHRISTMAS GOAL-FEST
On Boxing Day 1963, 66 goals were scored in the First Division of the Football League, still a record for the top flight of English football. The scores were: Blackpool 1 Chelsea 5; Burnley 6 Manchester United 1; Fulham 10 Ipswich Town 1; Leicester City 2 Everton 0; Liverpool 6 Stoke City 1; Nottingham Forest 3 Sheffield United 3; Sheffield Wednesday 3 Bolton Wanderers 0; West Bromwich Albion 4 Tottenham Hotspur 4; West Ham United 2 Blackburn Rovers 8; Wolves 3 Aston Villa 3.

No train, but one plane and several automobiles
One long journey for one very short career

S triker Billy Jervis did not have what one could consider a 'career' in the Football League. He played only one game, in fact – and he was very fortunate (or not, depending on your viewpoint) to have recorded even that.

In the summer of 1961 Jervis was transferred from First Division Blackburn Rovers, for whose first team he had never played, to Gillingham of the Fourth Division.

On Monday, 9 October that year, he set off with the rest of the Gillingham team for an evening match at Barrow, 245 miles (395km) away. The Gills planned to catch a 9.05am train from Euston that would have got them to Barrow, whose ground had no floodlights, one hour before the scheduled 5.15pm kick-off. But the coach taking them to the railway station was delayed and they missed their train.

The next train would not arrive in Barrow until after kick-off time,

and with road travel not an option in those pre-motorway days, Gillingham took the unusual decision of making the journey by air. Alas, what few scheduled flights there were to the north of England were full, so the Kent club chartered a private aircraft to take them to Blackpool, from where they completed the final 82 miles (132km) in a fleet of taxis.

The game started almost half an hour late and by the 76th minute, Barrow were winning 7-0, which was hardly surprising given Gillingham's

disrupted day. But now the skies were darkening rapidly and even though the Holker Street training lights were switched on, the referee abandoned the game because of bad light.

Unusually, the Football League ruled that the result should stand, which was a relief to Billy Jervis. He lost his place for the next match and never appeared in the Football League again. In July 1962, he was released and went to play for non-League Stalybridge Celtic.

Pulled muscle or playing badly? Bring on the sub
But injury-faking footballers prompt a rule change

I t is often an heroic scene: an injured player returning to the fray, perhaps his head swathed in a bloodstained bandage or his thigh heavily strapped, to do his best for his team. It was also a dilemma. How much further injury might be caused by sending back on to the pitch a player with, say, a torn muscle or a pulled hamstring? Not to mention the spoiling of hitherto well-balanced football matches – including seven out of ten FA Cup Finals between 1952 and 1961.

In 1965 the Football League decided to do something about it: by a vote of 39 clubs to ten, the League introduced a rule that allowed for one substitute player per match to replace an injured colleague.

Thus, on 21 August 1965 Kevin Peacock of Charlton Athletic became the first substitute to be introduced in a Football League match when he replaced his team's injured goalkeeper, Mike Rose, after only 11 minutes' play at Bolton. It should be noted that Peacock did not actually take over in goal; it was left to Charlton's John Hewie to don the green jersey while Peacock went into an outfield position and the team was reshuffled. Later the same day Bobby Knox of Barrow became the first substitute to score a goal when he netted against Wrexham. He was also reputedly the first substitute goalkeeper to save a penalty, against Doncaster Rovers.

The fact that Mike Rose had been injured was never in doubt. Why else would a team choose to take off its goalkeeper? That season, however, there were several instances where underperforming players suddenly and mysteriously developed a heavy limp. The recently retired Tottenham Hotspur and Northern Ireland player, Danny Blanchflower, suggested that any player who had been so replaced

without good reason should be banned from playing in his team's next match.

The Football League took a more practical view: for the following season a substitute was allowed for any reason, injury or tactical, and nowadays as many as three are allowed per game at any time in most football competitions.

Kevin Peacock, though, wasn't the first sub to be used in a big football match. Indeed, the first use of a substitute in international football dates back as far as 15 April 1899 when, at very short notice, Wales discovered that their goalkeeper, Jimmy Trainer, could not play against Scotland at Wrexham. A local amateur player, one Alf Pugh, guarded the Wales goal for the first 30 minutes before Sam Gillam of Wrexham FC replaced him.

Stan Mortensen of Blackpool scored 23 goals in 25 peacetime matches for England but his international debut came as a substitute for Wales in wartime. A few minutes after the start of a match at Wembley in September 1943, Ivor Powell, the Queen's Park Rangers

wing-half, suffered a fractured collarbone. The Welsh had no 12th man so all eyes fell on Mortensen, England's only reserve. 'I was so excited that I stood up on the touchline and started to pull off my RAF tunic in full view of the huge crowd,' he said later. Led away to get changed in a less public place, Mortensen returned to lay on two goals which reduced the Welsh deficit to 4–3 before England scored four more without reply.

The football war
When El Salvador and Honduras went into battle for real

El Salvador and Honduras were never the best of neighbours. But when they met in a World Cup playoff match in June 1969 it took the expression 'pitched battle' to hitherto unseen heights – or depths.

By the late 1960s there were an estimated 300,000 peasant farmers from tiny El Salvador cultivating land in the bigger Honduras. Their presence had been resented by Honduras for a decade.

On 30 April 1969 they were given 30 days to return to their homeland.

Unfortunately, the countries were also in the same World Cup sub-group, along with the USA and Haiti. Haiti won a two-legged tie against the USA with hardly anyone outside those countries noticing. For El Salvador and Honduras, however, there was no hiding place. The first leg of their tie took place at Tegucigalpa on 8 June 1969. On the eve of the game the Honduran hosts kept their visitors awake by playing loud music and letting off fireworks. On the day of the match there was rioting and an 18-year-old El Salvadoran fan, Amelia Bolaños, reportedly shot herself dead after watching on television as her team lost 1-0.

A week later, in San Salvador, the Honduran players received similar all-night treatment, and during the playing of the national anthems a dirty dishcloth was raised instead of the Honduran flag. Two visiting fans were injured, hundreds from both sides rioted, and El Salvador won 2-0.

Would this problem ever go away? Now there had to be a third match. The day after the second game, tens of thousands of El Salvadoran peasants were forced over the border, back to a country where they had nowhere to live. On 28 June, El Salvador broke off diplomatic relations with Honduras. Two days later, the nations met again at a football match, this time in neutral Mexico City where 1,700 Mexican police watched over 15,000 spectators in a stadium that could hold eight times that many.

For the record, the El Salvador team won 3-2 after extra-time to set up yet another play-off, this time against Haiti, whom they beat (that also took three matches) to go to the 1970 Finals in Mexico. Meanwhile, their country was about to go to war proper with Honduras. The conflict lasted four days before the Organisation of American States negotiated a cease-fire, which took effect on 20 July. Some call it the '100-Hour War'. More generally it is known as the 'Football War'.

Don't mention the World Cup ball
Tracked down after 30 years

It is well known that during the run-up to the 1966 World Cup finals the trophy was stolen and that it was a humble mongrel dog called Pickles who became a national hero when he sniffed it out of a suburban hedge in South London. Poor old Pickles didn't have long to enjoy his new-found fame. The following year he choked to death after his lead snagged on a fallen tree while he was chasing a cat.

But what about the ball which was used in England's extra-time 4-2 Wembley victory over West Germany? Custom dictates – and most right thinking people would surely agree – that it should have been presented to hat-trick legend Geoff Hurst. Well, eventually it was. But not for 30 years.

When the final whistle sounded at Wembley on 30 July 1966 the German midfielder Helmut Haller picked up the ball – 'It just rolled to me... how could I steal it?' – and stuffed it up his shirt. Haller gave it

to his son for the boy's fifth birthday. Over the years several world stars, including Pelé and Eusébio, signed it. But most of the time it lay undisturbed in the Hallers' loft.

Until 1996, that is, when several British newspapers and a football magazine campaigned to find the ball for its 'rightful' owner. Virgin boss Richard Branson, together with Eurostar, stumped up £70,000 between them, and with plenty of wartime metaphors in the headlines, the ball returned to London on 26 April. Hurst was photographed with it while the Germans were persuaded to hand the £70,000 to charity. It's perhaps best left to the *Daily Mirror* headline to round it off: 'They think it's all over – it is now'.

NOT YET OVER THE JIMMY HILL

Player, manager, union leader, pundit – Jimmy Hill has done it all. On 16 September 1972 Dennis Drewitt suffered torn ligaments while running the line in the Arsenal–Liverpool match at Highbury. With no reserve officials present in those days, the game was in danger of being abandoned when the football personality, who was a qualified referee, answered a public address appeal for a volunteer. Hill had been at the match as a spectator but donned a tracksuit to save the day.

True double sportsman
First-class football and cricket on the same day

The days when it was possible to be both a professional footballer and a professional cricketer have long gone. The generous overlapping of the seasons has seen to that. One of the last of this sturdy breed of dual sportsmen was a real 'Roy of the Rovers' figure.

In September 1975 he pulled off a unique feat, not only by becoming the only player ever to play League football and first-class cricket on the

same day but by playing in a Football League match in between scoring a century in the County Cricket Championship.

Chris Balderstone signed for Huddersfield Town in 1958. In June 1965 he was transferred to Carlisle United for £7,000. As a cricketer he made his first-class debut for Yorkshire in 1961 before moving to Leicestershire ten years later.

On Monday, 15 September 1975, Balderstone was 51 not out at close of play against Derbyshire at Chesterfield. Waiting to drive him to play for his new club, Doncaster Rovers, was the club's manager, Stan Anderson. Less than an hour later, Balderstone was turning out against Brentford in the Fourth Division. He helped his team to a 1-1 draw before resuming his innings at Chesterfield the following morning, going on to make 116 to help Leicestershire win

the Championship for the first time in their history.

Grounds of appeal
Football and cricket generally good neighbours

When on 29 December 1923 Darlington found their pitch at the Feethams frost-bound, they were not to be daunted. They simply switched their Third Division North match against Chesterfield to the adjacent cricket field where a crowd of 5,675 saw Bill Hooper score both their goals in a 2-1 victory.

When it came to neighbourliness, football and cricket often made happy bedfellows, although conditions were not always perfect. Before they moved to the Baseball Ground in 1895, Derby County shared the County Ground, Derby, with Derbyshire CCC. The pitch was perfect.

England international Steve Bloomer once recalled: 'We had no high-falutin' gadgets but we did have plenty of fresh air and cold water.'

Preston North End and Wales goalkeeper Jimmy Trainer always wore a brown-paper waistcoat to keep out the chill wind that always seemed to be blowing at Derby, while another Derby player, Jimmy Methven, remembered the dressing-room stove: 'When the lid was off, it had a flavour that would have made mustard gas feel shy.'

But Bramall Lane was perhaps the best dual football-cricket venue. Sheffield United FC and Yorkshire CCC alternated until August 1973, when the final County Championship match, against Leicestershire, was played there. Then the South Stand was built on part of the former cricket ground, finally enclosing the football ground on all four sides.

Following the loss of cricket at Bramall Lane, the last ground to host both Football League and County Championship matches was the County Ground at Northampton. Northampton Town moved in to

share the cricket ground upon their formation in 1897. Unhappily, the football pitch at the County Ground was reputed to be the worst playing surface in the Football League, no doubt due largely to it being used as a spectator area and car park during the cricket season. The last Football League match was played there on Tuesday, 11 October 1994 when Mansfield Town won a Fourth Division game 3-0. Four days later, Northampton Town drew 1-1 with Barnet in their first League match at the new Sixfields Stadium.

FASTEST OWN-GOAL IN LEAGUE HISTORY

On 3 January 1977 Cambridge United kicked off a Fourth Division game at Torquay United. Ian Seddon lofted the ball into the Torquay penalty area, and home defender Pat Kruse headed it past his own goalkeeper. Six seconds had elapsed. It was the fastest own-goal in Football League history. Torquay's Phil Sandercock later diverted the ball into his own net, so Torquay scored all the goals in the 2-2 draw.

On 20 March 1976, however, Aston Villa's Chris Nicholl had achieved that feat all on his own: two own-goals for Leicester City and two for his own team.

Whistle down the win
Fulham's missing 78 seconds

It was the final day of the 1982-83 season and the equation was simple: Fulham needed victory at Derby to stand any chance of winning promotion to the First Division; Derby needed all the points to be sure of avoiding relegation to the Third.

On the morning of the match, senior officers met at Derby's main police station. The aim was clear: to protect Fulham supporters. Given what was at stake for both clubs, Derby fans' long-established tradition of invading the pitch at the end of the last home game of the season appeared to threaten additional security problems.

So the briefing was quite clear. A pitch invasion was inevitable; fans would swarm over the Baseball Ground fences. And as the police would be powerless to prevent them, the best thing to do would be to unlock the fencing gates at the final whistle, let the home fans on to the playing area to cheer off their heroes for another season, and instead deploy men, dogs and horses around the Fulham enclosure, thus protecting visiting supporters.

There were 14 minutes remaining when Bobby Davison put Derby ahead with a brilliant goal. With 12 minutes to play, home fans began to climb over the fences. That was when

the order was given: 'Open the gates.'

Within seconds, one complete side of the Baseball Ground had spectators pushed right up to the touchline. This vital football match was becoming a farce. On at least two occasions, a home supporter tripped a Fulham player. It was difficult to comprehend what was happening.

Then referee Ray Chadwick gave a long blast on his whistle. To the crowd, and probably to the players, it signalled the end of the game and several thousand spectators now poured on to the pitch. Players and officials struggled to the sanctuary of the dressing rooms, although not before Fulham's Robert Wilson had been kicked by a spectator.

Then came news from the referee's room. He had simply whistled for offside. There were still 78 seconds to play. After about 15 minutes, however, it was obvious that it would be impossible to clear the pitch and play out the remaining time. Chadwick announced that he had abandoned the game.

Fulham were furious. They wanted the game replayed. At their appeal hearing at FA headquarters

at London's Lancaster Gate their manager, Malcolm Macdonald, produced at least one example where a club had scored twice in the last 78 seconds to turn a losing scoreline into a winning one. But the counter-argument was that it would be impossible to recreate the conditions of that final Saturday of the season. For one thing, thanks to other results, Derby now knew that, whatever the outcome, they were safe.

As he waited for the verdict, Macdonald was already making plans. Fulham's nearest rivals, Leicester City, had only managed to draw their last match. The Cottagers would win the restaged Derby game and go up along with Queen's Park Rangers and Wolves. He looked genuinely devastated when the inevitable pronouncement came, seeing it as a triumph of expediency over principle, and a victory for hooliganism. In that last point, he was probably right.

FROM ZERO BUT NOT TO HEROES

When Chesterfield visited Gillingham for a Third Division match on 5 September 1987 they had still to concede a goal after four League matches. After failing to score in their opening two matches, Gillingham had just recorded their second highest League score at the Priestfield Stadium, an 8-1 victory over Southend United. Who would buckle first? Gillingham beat Chesterfield 10-0.

Hang on while we look for a bomb
The IRA not keen on football

I t was a bleak afternoon as Birmingham City supporters trudged towards St Andrew's on Saturday, 7 December 1985. The home side were looking for their first win since late September. Their previous eight games had brought seven consecutive First Division defeats and just one draw. True, this day's visitors, Watford FC, were looking for their first win for eight weeks, yet still there was little room for Birmingham fans to suppose that recovery was just around the corner.

After 44 minutes this still looked to be the case. But in the final minute of a first half in which Watford had made all the running, it was Birmingham who took the lead when Andy Kennedy was tripped and Billy Wright drove home the penalty. Birmingham's joy was short-lived. Four minutes into the second half some slipshod defending left Watford legend Luther Blissett with yards of space to turn and volley home an equalising goal. Thereafter, this hitherto unremarkable but now well-balanced game ebbed and flowed until, in the 62nd minute, something astonishing happened: a police officer strode on to the pitch. The officer ignored the play going on around him and caught up with referee Neil Ashey. Next minute, the match official was rounding up the players and shepherding them off the field and out of the ground.

In the stands and on the terraces police and stewards were doing the same with 7,000 bewildered spectators.

Public address announcements appealed for calm, but spectators had no clue as to what they might indeed panic about.

Eventually word filtered through that the club had received a credible IRA bomb threat. Several similar threats had been phoned to First Division clubs that day and the rest had all carried on. But Birmingham still vividly remembered the IRA bomb that had killed 21 people and injured 182 others at the city's Mulberry Bush pub in November 1974.

The extraordinary thing was, however, that the football match was not abandoned. For an hour, spectators milled around outside as police checked the now empty stadium. Satisfied that there was no explosive device in the ground, they then allowed fans to be readmitted and the game to be restarted.

Birmingham City's concentration was affected most. Eight minutes after the resumption of play, Watford went ahead through Worrell Sterling. That was how it finished – 2-1 to Watford, who began a run of good results that

would take them to mid-table safety.

In contrast, Birmingham won only three more matches that season and were relegated.

From salad cream to stray dogs
Football's freak injuries

Before the start of the 1993-94 season Southampton goalkeeper Dave Beasant had a red face – and a sore foot – following a confrontation with a bottle of salad cream. Beasant knocked over the bottle and in attempting to cushion its fall with his foot he damaged a tendon and missed the first eight weeks of the season.

Beasant isn't the only professional footballer to have suffered a freak injury. The list seems endless but here are a few: Tottenham Hotspur's former Danish international Alan Nielsen missed several matches after his daughter prodded him in the eye, while Coventry City midfielder Youssef Chippo was similarly injured by team-mates after celebrating a goal against Preston North End.

After scoring the winning goal in the 1993 Littlewoods Cup Final against Sheffield Wednesday, Arsenal's Steve Morrow was also the victim of over-enthusiastic celebrations when Tony Adams hoisted Morrow high into the air, only to drop him and break the Northern Ireland international's shoulder.

But perhaps the most bizarre – and life-changing – injury was suffered by Brentford goalkeeper Chic Brodie. In a match at Colchester in November 1970 a stray dog found its way on to the pitch and collided with the goalkeeper, shattering his kneecap and ending his full-time professional career.

FRED WASN'T DEAD AFTER ALL

What did Congleton Town supporter Fred Cope and American author Mark Twain have in common? Not a lot, admittedly, except that reports of both their deaths were greatly exaggerated. On 27 February 1993 Congleton and Rossendale players were just about to observe a minute's silence to honour Congleton's oldest fan when the 85-year-old former ambulance driver ambled into the ground to watch the HFS Loans League match. After reading his own obituary in the match programme and feeling lucky, Fred bought a raffle ticket – and won £10. Congleton were so relieved that they went on to win 6-1.

'Bambi on ice'
How the wool was pulled over Graeme Souness's eyes

When Southampton manager Graeme Souness thought that he'd received a telephone call from the 1995 FIFA World Footballer of the Year, George Weah, recommending Weah's cousin as someone who could help the Saints, he didn't think twice about offering a trial to one Ali Dia.

Unfortunately, it wasn't Weah who made the call. And far from being a potential world-beater, the 30-year-old Dia – who was absolutely no relation to Weah – turned out to be one of the worst footballers ever to 'grace' the top of the English game.

The reserve team match against Arsenal in which Dia should have made his debut was postponed due to a waterlogged pitch. Amazingly, without the manager ever having seen him play, he then found himself named as a substitute for Southampton's home FA Premiership fixture against Leeds United on 23 November 1996.

In the 32nd minute, England international Matthew Le Tissier suffered an injury, and on came Ali Dia in his place. He lasted only 21 minutes before the substitute was himself substituted. Le Tissier later said: 'His performance was almost comical. He ran around the pitch like Bambi on ice; it was very embarrassing. I don't think he realised

what position he was supposed to be in. I don't even know if he spoke English. In the end he got himself subbed because he was that bad.'

The original call, in which Dia had been described as a Senegalese international who had played for Paris St Germain, had apparently been made by one of Dia's fellow university students. Dia had played in the lower reaches of French and German football and been turned away by Port Vale, Bournemouth and Gillingham before making one appearance for non-League team Blyth Spartans.

He was quickly released by Southampton and played eight times for non-League Gateshead before graduating in business studies in 2001 from Northumbria University. In 2007 *The Times* newspaper voted him number one in their list of 'The 50 Worst Footballers'.

NOT HIS FINEST HOUR

Poor Jonathan Woodgate. After joining Real Madrid from Newcastle United in August 2004, injuries prevented him from making his competitive Spanish debut until 22 September 2005. And what a debut it was: against Athletic Bilbao he scored an own-goal before being sent off in the 65th minute. In 2007 Woodgate was voted the worst signing by a Spanish club in the 21st century.

Jonathan Woodgate

PEOPLE IN FOOTBALL GROUNDS SHOULDN'T THROW CELERY

Gillingham FC has few claims to fame, but in 1996 it was the first League club to ban celery. Supporters had been hiding sticks of celery down their trousers before bombarding the Gills' 16st 6lb (104kg) goalkeeper, Jim Stannard, with the vegetable, all preceded by the 'Celery Song', complete with saucy lyrics. The club's programme editor explained: 'Our goalkeeper is the heaviest player in the League. A lot of celery was thrown and, inevitably, some went in his direction.'

The Gold Chain Derby
It's a good thing Mr T doesn't play football

'We was robbed!' It is a common enough complaint from managers, players and fans whenever a refereeing decision goes against them. But when Uruguay's top two teams, Club Atlético Peñarol and Club Nacional, met in a local derby match, a real theft was committed on the pitch – by one player upon another.

The Montevideo rivals' clash is the longest running senior derby match outside the British Isles. Since the clubs first met in September 1900, they have played each other more than 500 times. But it was a match between the two sides in 1991 that saw a crime committed and the Montevideo derby acquire a new name.

There was the usual pushing and jostling when Nacional prepared to take a corner, with Peñarol defenders eager to put pressure on the attacking side. And when the ball came across, the foul deed was done: Peñarol's Jorge Goncalves ripped off one of several gold chains hanging around the neck of Nacional's Panamanian international, Julio Dely Valdes – and stuffed it down his sock.

Valdes, used to being jostled and already weighed down with jewellery,

apparently did not notice, but the incident was picked up by television cameras and when the players trooped into the dressing room at the end of the game, police were waiting to arrest Goncalves.

His defence was rather weak – 'I don't know what I was thinking' – but after returning the chain, he was released without charge, and since that day matches between Uruguay's oldest rivals have been known as the Gold Chain Derby.

Teams that wanted to score against themselves
Crazy rule that saw football become farce

It's obvious, surely: the object of a football match is to score goals, goals against your opponents that is. The team that does it most will win the game. However, when Barbados met Grenada in a Shell Caribbean Cup match in 1994, that logic was turned upside down.

When the teams went into the final match in their group, Barbados needed to win by two clear goals in order to advance to the Final.

Anything less and Grenada would go through. In the case of a draw after 90 minutes, then extra time would be played. The first goal scored in extra time would be a 'golden goal' and win the game. And it would count for two. It was a bizarre ruling and it made for a bizarre end to this particular football match.

When Barbados took an early 2-0 lead it seemed that they would be playing in the Final, but with seven minutes remaining, Grenada pulled a goal back. The 2-1 scoreline spelled disaster for Barbados. They needed to score a goal – any goal.

With so little time remaining and Grenada now playing ultra-defensively with every player behind the ball, one Barbadian decided that his team's best chance of success was to take the game into extra time. Then Grenada would have to come out on the attack and Barbados would have a better chance of scoring that golden goal, which would count as two goals and see them through. So he did no more than shoot the ball past his own goalkeeper to make it 2-2.

Grenada now needed to score a goal – at either end – to avoid extra time and to go through to the Final. So they turned around and headed for their own net.

Then the farce really began. The Barbadians rushed to defend their opponents' goal until the

whistle sounded to signal extra time. Four minutes into the extra period, Barbados again found the back of the net, the correct net this time. The scoreline was now 4-2 (remember the golden goal counted double) and Barbados had their two-goal victory margin.

The Grenadians were furious. Their manager, James Clarkson, said: 'I feel cheated. The person who came up with these rules must be a candidate for the madhouse. The game should never be played with so many players on the field so confused. Our players did not even know which direction to attack – our goal or their goal. In football, you are supposed to score against your opponents in order to win, not for them.' Classic.

When team-mates come to blows
Charlton's pair of strikers took it literally

There were only five minutes left to play in the FA Cup third round match between Charlton Athletic and Maidstone United at

The Valley on 9 January 1979. The score was 1-1 and both sets of players were becoming frustrated.

Maidstone had taken the lead after 13 minutes and it wasn't until the 77th that Mike Flanagan had equalised for Charlton. Now Flanagan played the ball through to his bearded team-mate, Derek Hales. But before Hales could collect the pass, up went a linesman's flag. He was offside.

Hales was not pleased. In fact he was angry. So angry that he began to remonstrate with Flanagan, whom he said should have made the pass earlier. Flanagan said something to the effect that he'd been playing Hales through all season, not that it had come to much. Swear words were exchanged. And then Hales and Flanagan began fighting. Hales lashed out first, then Flanagan responded. Referee Brian Martin had no alternative: he sent off both players.

The 13,457 crowd, not to mention the rest of the players, were stunned.

Three days later Charlton sacked Hales but retained his registration. Flanagan was fined £250. On 1 February, Flanagan handed in a transfer request. Four days later Hales

rejected a transfer to Cardiff City. Four days after that he was reinstated and fined two weeks' wages. Later that month, Flanagan walked out on the club over the handling of his transfer request.

Flying chicken wings
*Italian love affair ruined
by a plate of food*

G rimsby Town supporters have never been used to their club signing players with exotic names and from exotic backgrounds, but when the Mariners secured the services of Ivano Bonetti in 1995, he soon became a firm favourite with supporters, not least because he paid part of his own transfer fee.

Bonetti had seen service with such famous Italian football names as Juventus, Atalanta, Bologna, Sampdoria and Torino. An American management company held the ultimate rights to his 'services and image' and wanted £100,000 to sell him on. Under FIFA regulations, Grimsby were not allowed to deal with the company and, indeed, they probably could not have afforded him anyway, but £50,000 was raised by the club's supporters, with Bonetti himself providing the other £50,000.

It was a love affair completed when, in November 1995, Bonetti scored the winning goal against West Bromwich Albion, a club managed by former Grimsby Town boss Alan Buckley and whose team contained several former Grimsby players.

On 10 February 1996, however, things turned sour with Grimsby losing 3-2 at Luton Town. Only a month earlier, Grimsby had beaten the same opponents 7-1 in the FA Cup. Now the Mariners' manager Brian Laws apparently felt that Bonetti had not tried hard enough. In the dressing room after the game he threw a plate of chicken wings at the player, fracturing his cheekbone.

At the season's end Bonetti was given a free transfer to Tranmere

Rovers. Laws lasted at Grimsby a little longer, until November of the following season. At the start of 1997-98, Bonetti moved on to Crystal Palace before returning to Italy.

No petrol money, no players
The team that went on strike over travelling expenses

You would have thought that all was well in the world of Weymouth FC on the first day of 1983. The Alliance Premier League club had won its previous nine matches. The visit to Maidstone United on New Year's Day was a vital affair with both clubs battling for the championship.

However, behind the scenes all was not well. Weymouth had a bank overdraft of £50,000 – small beer today but a small fortune in 1983 – and the club was losing £700 every week of the season. Economies therefore had to be made.

Ten of the players lived in the Bournemouth area, 37 miles (60km) from Weymouth. To transport them to matches and to training by car the club was paying £200 every week. It was calculated that bringing them in as a group in a mini-bus would save £100 a week. The players were not impressed. They felt that this was a breach of their contracts.

When on 1 January 1983 the mini-bus turned up at Ferndown, 8 miles (13km) north of Bournemouth, to pick up the players to take them to Maidstone's Athletic Ground, there was no-one to be seen apart from the Weymouth manager, Stuart Morgan. The game had to be postponed for lack of players.

The footballers' strike lasted 48 hours before Weymouth beat Bath City at home to record their tenth successive victory. The club had ended the industrial action by shelving the mini-bus plan and agreeing to go to arbitration where most of the disaffected players agreed to an increase of £15 in their weekly wage in lieu of travelling expenses. However, that was not the end of the matter.

The Alliance Premier League fined Weymouth £100 for failing to fulfil the fixture, and ordered them to pay Maidstone United £895 in expenses, and £182 towards the cost of the hearing. Controversially the league also docked Weymouth ten points, a penalty that dropped them down the table and out of the championship race.

Weymouth appealed to the Football Association. By the time of the hearing in March they had won only one of their previous six matches. The FA ordered the fines and costs to stand but overruled the deduction of points and ordered the Maidstone game to be rearranged. Maidstone won that 3-0 but missed the title by one point, while Weymouth, their season disrupted beyond rescue, finally dropped to seventh.

THREE GOALS, THREE DIFFERENT GOALKEEPERS

When West Ham United defender Alvin Martin scored a hat-trick in the Hammers' 8-1 win over Newcastle United at Upton Park on 21 April 1986, each of his goals was scored against a different goalkeeper. The first went past Martin Thomas who was later injured, the second beat his replacement, Chris Hedworth, and the third came when Peter Beardsley had taken over between the posts.

Billy Dodds

Only one team in Tallinn – and they're Scottish
Long way to go for three seconds

When Scotland travelled to play Estonia in a World Cup qualifying match in Tallinn on 9 October 1996, it looked an unremarkable enough event. Both teams had failed to get off to a winning start in their campaigns and now only one point separated them in the Group 4 table. It would,

though, go down as one of the most memorable fixtures in World Cup history, even though it lasted for only three seconds – and with only one team on the pitch.

On the eve of the match, Scotland's players trained under floodlights at the Kadriorg Stadium. As soon as they stepped on to the playing area, the Scots looked unhappy. Their concern was the inconsistency of the floodlights which cast some areas of the pitch into half-shadow while in other parts, most notably in one of the goalmouths, low level lamps glared into the players' eyes.

The Scots complained to the official FIFA observer, Jean-Marie Gantenbein of Luxembourg, who overruled their objections and said that the match would kick-off at 6.45pm as scheduled. However, Gantenbein began to have second thoughts and early the next morning, after contacting FIFA bosses in Zurich, he ruled that the match would be brought forward to 3pm.

Now it was the Estonians' turn to get unhappy. Their president, Aiver Pohlak, pointed out that this would present the team with a logistical nightmare. Some of their players were part-time footballers and would be at work that afternoon. Others were at a training camp, 62 miles (100km) away at Kethna. And what about the supporters? They would also be at work. There was one other major problem: the Estonians had a TV contract that depended on an evening start.

Pohlak said: 'We shall leave our headquarters at 4pm as scheduled for a 6.45pm kick-off. We know that the Scots will have been and gone by then and there will be no game today. But we do think the Scottish

FA have been very, very unfair to us.'

Sure enough, when Scotland lined up for a 3pm start, there was no sign of the Estonian team. Billy Dodds kicked off and passed to John Collins, and then Yugoslavian referee Miroslav Radoman abandoned the game that had lasted for only three seconds.

On 11 February 1997, the match was replayed at a neutral venue, the two countries drawing 0-0 in Monaco. Scotland eventually qualified for the finals, Estonia did not, and the fixture is best remembered for the comic element introduced by Scotland's travelling supporters who sang: 'One team in Tallinn, there's only one team in Tallinn.'

The green parrot given a red card
Me-Tu's touchline ban

There was something strange going on during the Hertfordshire Senior Centenary Trophy match between Hertford Heath and Hatfield Town in January 2009, and it wasn't the football that was being played.

The second half had been under way for ten minutes when a whistle sounded. Both teams stopped, surprised, because as far as they could see there had been no foul or injury, no interruption to normal play.

Referee Gary Bailey was as confused as anyone. He hadn't blown his whistle. So he signalled for play to continue. Then the whistle sounded again. And it kept on sounding.

There was obviously a mischief-maker among the 150 hardy fans lining the touchline. Mr Bailey was determined to identify the culprit. So imagine his surprise when someone pointed to a green parrot.

Irene Kerrigan's Senegal parrot Me-Tu was a regular at Hertford Heath's home fixtures. But now he was demonstrating a new-found ability: mimicking the referee's whistle. Said ref Bailey: 'I've never known anything like it in my football career. It was a big game and there were quite a lot of people there. This woman was standing right by the touchline and suddenly she unveiled a big cage with this big green parrot in it.

'I didn't mind at first. But then every time I blew my whistle the bird made exactly the same sound. The players stopped so I had to ask her to move the parrot. It was bizarre. The crowd were laughing, but in the end, there was only one thing for it.'

Despite Me-Tu's touchline ban, Mrs Kerrigan, who lives near the ground, was defiant. She told the *Daily Mail*: 'He loves football and I'll take him back down there again next Saturday.' Hopefully with his beak taped shut.

Referees who red card themselves
When match officials lose it

When Peterborough North End goalkeeper Richard McGaffin complained vociferously about the goal that he had just conceded in a Peterborough Sunday League Second Division match against Royal Mail AYL in January 2005, he might have expected to get into hot water with referee Andy Wain.

What the keeper didn't expect was that the match official would throw down his whistle and untuck his shirt before marching up to eyeball him.

Fortunately, referee Wain soon realised that he had overstepped the mark. So he sent himself off. But before he did so, with no other referee available to take over, he abandoned the game.

The 39-year-old official later admitted he should have stayed at home that day. 'With hindsight I should never have officiated,' he said. 'It was totally unprofessional. If a player did that I would send him off,

so I had to go. I heard the keeper say: "It's always the bloody same with you, ref – we never get anything." It was the last straw, but fortunately I came to my senses.' The Northamptonshire FA later banned Wain for 35 days and fined him £50.

In 1998, however, referee Melvin Sylvester went one step further by attacking a player in the Andover and District Sunday League match between Southampton Arms and Hurstbourne Tarrant British Legion. 'I was sorely provoked,' explained Sylvester afterwards. 'I punched him several times after he had pushed me from behind. He then swore. I couldn't take any more. I blew my top.'

Sylvester sent himself off but this time the game was able to continue, as a spectator took charge. Sylvester was fined £20 and banned for six weeks by the Hampshire Football Association. After the verdict he said: 'I'm furious. The disciplinary committee have got their priorities all wrong.'

LIKE FATHER, LIKE SON
On 23 May 2009 Clive Oliver refereed the League Two Play-off Final between Gillingham and Shrewsbury Town at Wembley. The following day his son, Michael, refereed the League One Play-off Final between Millwall and Scunthorpe United at the same ground. On 23 August 2005 the pair had become the first father and son to officiate together in a senior match in England when Michael ran the line for his dad at the Rotherham United-Port Vale Carling Cup tie.

A few of football's marked men
Naughty boys who played with electronic tags

More than a few top-class footballers have found themselves behind prison bars for a number of reasons unconnected with the game, but Duncan Ferguson goes down in history as the first British professional player to be jailed for an incident during a match.

In a Scottish League match at Ibrox between Rangers and Raith Rovers on 16 April 1994 Ferguson head-butted visiting defender John McStay. Ferguson avoided a dismissal because referee Kenny Clark and his linesmen missed the incident but television cameras caught it and the player was subsequently charged with assault. He was found guilty and as it was his fourth similar conviction – the others had involved a police officer, a fisherman and a Heart of Midlothian supporter – he was sentenced to three months' imprisonment. Ferguson eventually served 44 days in Glasgow's Barlinnie prison in 1995, by which time he had become an Everton player.

In 2001, Ferguson was the victim of a burglary attempt by two men on his Liverpool home. They could have selected an easier target. The footballer detained one of them who subsequently spent three days in hospital. Both burglars were sentenced to 15 months' imprisonment for their foolhardy actions.

The first professional player to be jailed following an incident during a match in England was Barrow defender James Cotterill who received a four-month sentence after punching the Bristol Rovers player Sean Rigg during an FA Cup first-round match at Holker Street, Barrow, on 11 November 2006. The blow broke Rigg's jaw in two places. As with the Ferguson incident, the referee and his assistants did not see the offence but television cameras captured it. Cotterill was jailed on 11 January but released a month later and forced to wear an electronic tag for a further month.

Cotterill was also banned from football until March 2007 so the 'honour' of being the first footballer to play in a British professional match while wearing an electronic tag fell to Ipswich Town defender Gary Croft, who had been convicted of perverting the course of justice, and driving while disqualified.

After serving one quarter of a four-month sentence, Croft came on as a substitute against Swindon Town in a First Division match at Portman Road on 15 January 2000, with the tag clearly visible on his left ankle. In the early weeks following his release a 7pm-to-7am curfew had

also been imposed on the player so he could not play in evening matches.

The first player to appear in the FA Premier League while wearing an electronic tag was Birmingham City's Jermaine Pennant when he turned out against Tottenham Hotspur on 2 April 2005. Pennant had been released from prison after serving 30 days of a 90-day sentence for drink driving, driving while disqualified and driving without insurance. Pennant, who was on loan from Arsenal at the time, was also subject to a 7am-to-7pm curfew. In January 2011 it was reported that Pennant's £98,000 Porsche 911 Turbo car had been found apparently abandoned at a Spanish railway station after the player, who had moved to Stoke City, had forgotten that he owned it when playing for Real Zaragoza.

Duncan Ferguson

Going to the Match – it's expensive these days
Lowry's painting finds a home

I s it the ultimate piece of football memorabilia? The Professional Footballers' Association (PFA) obviously thought so when they paid £1,926,500 for L. S. Lowry's 1953 painting entitled *Going to the Match*.

The painting depicts supporters on their way to a football match at Burnden Park, the former home ground of Bolton Wanderers, close to where the artist lived.

When the players' union purchased the work of art at Sotheby's auction house in London in 1999, the PFA secretary, Gordon Taylor, said: 'It represents the heart and soul of the game and the anticipation of fans on their way to a match.'

It had been expected to sell for about £500,000. Taylor afterwards said: 'I would have liked it for a lot less than that, but it is the football picture, it captures all the atmosphere of the game.

'We wanted to keep the picture in football. It's always said that there's not enough literature and art surrounding the world's greatest game, so we are trying to build up a collection of memorabilia – caps, medals, jerseys – and good football pictures.

'Lowry did show an interest in the game. We want to keep it in the North West, where he came from, and we want it to be on display to the public.'

Taylor said that the painting would be loaned to the Salford Art Gallery and Museum before moving to the new Lowry Centre that April.

L. S. Lowry statue, Mottram

OOOPS! THE TRANSFER SCOOP THAT WASN'T

It seemed quite reasonable that FA Premiership giants Liverpool should want to sign a French Under-21 international left-back from AS Monaco for £3.5 million. And that was what **The Times** *and the* **News of the World,** *not to mention Liverpool's own official Clubcall line, reported in November 1999. Unfortunately the player, Didier Baptiste, existed only in the imagination of the scriptwriters of the Sky TV series* **Dream Team.** *There were red faces all round as a news agency was blamed for the misreporting.*

When Socrates played for Garforth

The Brazilian superstar who lit up (in) a small Yorkshire town

When Northern Counties East Football League club Garforth Town announced that they were about to sign the legendary Brazilian star, Socrates, most people thought it was an elaborate hoax.

The thought of the captain of the great Brazilian World Cup team of 1982 turning out for a Yorkshire non-League side was too ridiculous to be taken seriously.

But, sure enough, in November 2004 the 50-year-old Socrates made his debut against Tadcaster United. A crowd of 1,300 turned up, Garforth's biggest attendance for over 40 years.

Garforth's owner, Simon Clifford, a businessman with a series of football schools based on Brazilian coaching techniques, had persuaded Socrates to sign a one-month contract for the Yorkshire football minnows.

Clifford said later: 'He came on as a substitute but I decided not to play him in the next game because his warm-up had consisted of drinking two bottles of Budweiser and three cigarettes which we had in the changing rooms. I didn't think it was a good idea for him to carry on playing too much more, keen to do so though he was.'

Paying tribute to the Brazilian star after his death from severe septicaemia in December 2011, the man who brought Socrates to the backwoods of the English game said: 'In the early 1980s, when Brazil was under a military government, he was basically behind a democracy movement in the club... It wasn't so much what he did for football but for Brazilian society as a whole. His courage was immense.'

Long hair and earrings – banned!
They like their football strictly manly in Argentina and Nigeria

O ne evening while he was watching BBC television's *Match of the Day*, the great Liverpool manager Bill Shankly called to his wife, Nessie, to hurry from the kitchen so that she might look at the Derby County team featuring in the match highlights he was watching.

In the early 1970s long hair was *de rigueur* for professional footballers but Brian Clough's Derby team sported short haircuts, and Shankly wanted to show Nessie 'how smart they all look'.

So perhaps Liverpool's legendary team boss would have approved of the actions taken by

the Nigerian Football Association in September 2004 when it tried to deter young Nigerian footballers from wearing hair braids, dreadlocks and earrings.

One Nigerian FA administrator, Ahmed Lawan, went so far as to say that any player who arrived with an unusual hairdo should be prevented from entering the pitch: 'He should

be suspended for some years or even banned from playing football.'

The issue had come to light before elsewhere: in 1998, the Argentina coach Daniel Passarella had refused to pick Real Madrid midfielder Fernando Redondo unless the long-haired player visited the barber. Passarella said that players with flowing locks were distracted from their game by constantly rearranging their hair.

Then again he also banned earrings – and was quoted by Argentinean newspapers as saying that he did not want homosexuals in his team either. And this is what lay behind that Nigerian ruling: sports officials claimed that besides long hair being culturally unacceptable in their country, it also promoted homosexuality.

A leading government official from Nigeria's National Orientation Agency, Otunba Olusegun Runsewe, agreed. He was still agreeing seven years later when, in December 2011, he applauded the actions of national football coach Stephen Keshi who banned his players from wearing earrings. Runsewe, by now the

director-general of the Nigerian Tourism Development Corporation, said: 'Stephen Keshi's action is courageous and bold... I have always said that it is not cultural for men to be wearing women's apparel in Africa. It is a bad habit that people should not copy, especially by footballers that are hero-worshipped by our teaming youths. They should set an example.'

The great hijab debate
Olympic dreams shattered by head-covering ban

When in 2010 FIFA announced that it was planning to ban players from wearing any form of religious clothing or insignia during the 2012 London Olympics it spelled the end of the road for the hopes of Iran's women footballers.

Under the stricter Iranian rules, all women are required to cover their body head to toe, but the FIFA ruling meant that women footballers, who played in full tracksuits, could not wear the hijab. So a special scarf was designed that players wrapped tightly around their heads and necks. Alas, so far as FIFA was concerned even that broke its rules that banned the manifestation of religious symbols.

A puzzled Farideh Shojaei, head of women's affairs at Iran's football federation, told Reuters TV: 'We made the required corrections and played a match afterwards. We played again and were not prevented from doing so, and they didn't find anything wrong. That meant that there were no obstacles in our path, and that we could participate in the Olympics.'

But FIFA was adamant. It told Reuters: 'The decision in March 2010 which permitted that players be allowed to wear a cap that covers their head to the hairline, but does not extend below the ears to cover the neck, is still applicable.

'Despite initial assurances that the Iranian delegation understood this, the players came out wearing the hijab, and the head and neck totally covered, which was an infringement of the Laws of the Game. The match commissioner and match referee therefore decided to apply correctly the Laws of the Game, which ended in the match being abandoned.'

The match in question was a qualifier against Jordan and it was not abandoned; it was never even started. FIFA claimed that Iranian officials were 'informed thoroughly' before the match that the hijab scarf covering a women's neck was banned for safety reasons.

Mr Shojaei said that Iran's football federation chief, Ali Kafashian, 'took it to FIFA and showed it to Mr Sepp Blatter' to prove they were not in breach of conduct. 'In reality, this kit

is neither religious, nor political, nor will it harm a player.'

But FIFA would not budge and neither would the Iranian government, which refused to allow its female players to remove the hijab. Iran's opponents in the qualifying group for 2012 – Jordan, Vietnam, Thailand and Uzbekistan – were each awarded the respective matches by a 3–0 scoreline, and the Iranian women's Olympic dreams were over before they had properly begun.

BANNED FROM WATCHING FOOTBALL – EVEN ON TV

Life has often been difficult for female footballers. In Iran it is difficult even for females who simply want to watch a game. Already banned from entering stadiums, in November 2011 Iranian women found themselves forbidden even from viewing football matches on television in public screening rooms.

Why you should never leave before the end
Parents miss their son's moment of history

==========

Mary and Richard Hayter looked at their watches and decided that with only ten minutes remaining of the Division Two match between AFC Bournemouth and Wrexham at Dean Court on 24 February 2004, there was now no chance that their son, James, would be brought off the Bournemouth substitutes' bench.

The Isle of Wight ferry

So together with James's brother, Ben, they decided to leave to catch the ferry back to their home on the Isle of Wight, where the family's dogs were waiting. It was a decision that cost them the chance to see their son make history. Four minutes after the Hayters had left the ground, James was brought on. And in only 140 seconds he scored three times – the quickest hat-trick in Football League history.

Hayter, who touched the ball only four times as Bournemouth won 6-0, told the *Daily Telegraph* that he must have been inspired by the birth three days earlier of his son, Harris: 'Mum and Dad had been in the main stand watching the game. They came over earlier that day to spend some time with the baby.

'They told me they would probably leave early and so I thought there was a chance they had missed it. I feel really sorry for them after coming all this way. They didn't even see me get on as substitute. My dad was absolutely gutted but also really chuffed for me.'

Hayter's father, a retired hotelier, said: 'We waited for most of the match to see James but after the manager put on two subs we thought he would never get on. We decided to leave so we could make the 10.30pm ferry. If we had left later we would have been stuck in traffic in the car park.

'I switched on the radio and the commentator announced that James had just come on. But the next couple of minutes were just a blur. All I remember is the commentator shouting out James's name over and over again. I was going mad. I didn't know whether to laugh or cry.'

Club Chairman sees a UFO
But fails to spot the false messiah trying to take over his club

You might think that a man who once tried to buy Manchester United would himself have been wary of a 'messiah' coming to the rescue. But when Carlisle United chairman Michael Knighton was approached by Stephen Brown, who claimed to have made £6.3 million from the sale of a hotel complex in Spain and was now desperate to help save the Carlisle club, he was impressed.

It was in 1989 that Knighton, who had made money in the property market while still working as a schoolteacher, made a £20 million bid for Manchester United. To publicise his takeover attempt he went on to the Old Trafford pitch before the opening game of the season against Arsenal, and, dressed in full United kit, juggled the ball in front of 47,000 supporters. But Knighton's backers slowly melted away.

In retrospect it could have been the football sale of the century; in 2005 Manchester United was sold for £790 million. In the meantime, Knighton had taken over Carlisle United. Assuming control at Brunton Park in 1992, he declared that Carlisle would be a Premier League club within ten years. But, although they won the Third Division in 1995 and the Auto Windscreens Shield in 1997, they eventually hit hard times and looked likely to drop out of the Football League instead.

Enter Stephen Brown, the public face of a consortium apparently ready to take over the troubled Cumbrian club. A former Partick Thistle season

ticket holder, 47-year-old Brown intended to join United's new board as commercial director for a two-month trial before paying Knighton for his share of the club.

But doubts began to surface. It emerged that Brown had failed in a bid to buy Partick in 1998, and likewise in attempts to invest in Peebles and Selkirk rugby clubs, despite claiming to have won millions of pounds on the lottery.

'He came to us saying he wanted to invest great sums of money but, when we started discussing it in detail, he said he wasn't putting forward the money but was proposing a sponsorship scheme backed by friends,' former president of Selkirk, Norman Douglas, told *The Guardian*.

The newspaper reported that Brown appeared to live in an old people's home in Peebles, where his partner was a janitor; that he had been working as a barman in an Indian restaurant; that he had been barred from a Peebles hotel for causing 'serious trouble'; and that, far from driving a smart BMW, he owned only a battered Vauxhall Cavalier.

After Brown had failed to make

a payment of £250,000 for a 25 per cent stake in the club's parent company, CUFC Holdings Ltd, by Knighton's deadline, Knighton said: 'This man has caused horrendous embarrassment to me and the club. I have never been hoodwinked in my life. I usually pride myself on my ability to see straight through people.'

In September 2000 Knighton himself was disqualified from being a company director for five and a half years following an investigation into his business affairs. The disqualification related to Knighton's running of a private school that he owned via the same holding company, Knighton Holdings, through which he also owned Carlisle United. He eventually sold Carlisle United to Irish businessman John Courtenay in 2002.

Knighton was never popular with Carlisle supporters, especially after appointing himself as manager in 1998 and winning only 19 of the 68 games for which he was in charge. In 1996 he found himself publicly mocked after claiming that he and his wife, Rosemary, had seen a UFO. The local newspaper, the *Evening*

News and Star, broke the story with the headline: 'Knighton: Aliens Spoke To Me'.

As they set off from their Yorkshire home one afternoon in 1976, he and his wife had watched an apparently alien craft perform a range of 'impossible' aero-gymnastics. As the glowing UFO disappeared, he believed he had received a telepathic message urging him: 'Don't be afraid, Michael.'

After the story was published, he said: 'I made it perfectly clear to the reporter that it was not for publication. The damage has been done now and so I've decided to resign at the end of the season. I have a nine-year-old son and it's not fair for him to be ridiculed.'

The *Evening News and Star* followed up with a front-page article in which its editor, Keith Sutton, tendered an 'unreserved' though perhaps tongue-in-cheek apology. He said: 'Just because Michael Knighton has seen a UFO doesn't disqualify him from being a football club chairman.'

The Battle of Bramall Lane
Injuries, red cards and accusations fly

When West Bromwich Albion arrived at Bramall Lane on 16 March 2002 they were looking for victory against Sheffield United in order to maintain their ambition of promotion to the FA Premiership.

And when United's goalkeeper, Simon Tracey, was sent off after only nine minutes for handling the ball outside his penalty area, it seemed that Albion's task had suddenly become much easier.

His team already down to ten men, United manager Neil Warnock replaced an outfield player with substitute goalkeeper Wilko de Vogt, who could do nothing to prevent Scott Dobie's opening goal ten minutes later. When Derek McInnes made it 2-0 with less than half an hour remaining, it seemed that West Brom were heading straight for maximum points.

But then the game erupted. Warnock sent on his final two substitutes, Georges Santos and

Patrick Suffo. Two minutes later and both were heading for an early bath. Santos was sent off for a foul on Albion's Andy Johnson (the pair had a spot of 'previous'; the prior season Johnson, then at Nottingham Forest, had broken the Frenchman's cheekbone with a flying elbow). In the fracas that followed involving all 21 players, Suffo also received his marching orders, leaving Sheffield with only eight players.

In the 80th minute, Michael Brown left the pitch with an injury and when Robert Ullathorne followed him a couple of minutes later, Sheffield United were down to six players. The minimum number a team must have is seven players so referee Eddie Wolstenholme had no option but to abandon the game with West Brom leading 3-0.

Their manager, Gary Megson, fumed: 'I've been in professional football since 16 and I'm 42 now. I've never ever witnessed anything as disgraceful as that. There is no place for that in any game of football, let alone professional football. There will be no replay. If we are called back to Bramall Lane we shall kick

off and then walk off the pitch.'

Megson accused Warnock of faking the injuries to end the game but an investigation cleared the Blades' manager, although United were fined £10,000 and the result allowed to stand. Santos and Suffo never again played for Sheffield United, while West Brom finished the season in second place to win promotion.

Neil Warnock

The FA Cup tie that wouldn't die

Chesterfield and Droylsden just couldn't bear to say bye

When League Two club Chesterfield and Blue Square North side Droylsden were drawn in the second round of the 2008-09 FA Cup, no-one could have expected them to drag it out for so long.

In the first match at Saltergate the non-Leaguers were leading 1-0 at half-time when the game was abandoned because of fog.

The second attempt at Saltergate ended in a 2-2 draw with the game being held up for five minutes because of a disputed goal after Droylsden had put the ball out of play after an injury to their striker Carl Lamb. From the throw-in Chesterfield kept possession and took a 2-1 lead through Jack Lester. This was considered unsporting and eventually Chesterfield allowed Steve Halford to walk the ball through unchallenged to give the non-Leaguers a replay.

Alas, that ended in controversy when the floodlights at Droylsden's Butcher's Arms ground failed with Chesterfield winning 2-0 with only 19 minutes still to play. A fourth match was played two days before Christmas 2008 and this time Droylsden defender Sean Newton scored twice as the non-Leaguers beat ten-men Chesterfield, who had Jack Lester sent off, 2-1. Now Droylsden faced a third-round tie at Ipswich. Or so everyone thought.

Sean Newton

It was discovered that on 23 December, Newton should in fact have been serving a one-match ban. The FA expelled the non-Leaguers and reinstated Chesterfield.

However, this was far from the longest running FA Cup saga. In 1971, in the days before penalty competitions, Alvechurch and Oxford City took six attempts and 11 hours to find a winner in their fourth qualifying round tie.

ONE LONG SCILLY SEASON...

If you visit St Mary's, the largest of the Isles of Scilly, any Sunday between the end of October and the end of March, then you will probably find Garrison Gunners playing Woolpack Wanderers. In fact it would be surprising if you didn't, for they are the only members of the world's smallest football league. They meet 17 times each season in the Isles of Scilly League, and in case that isn't enough, there are also two cup competitions – both played over two legs, of course.

Manager for just ten minutes
Manages to see the funny side

When Leroy Rosenior returned to Torquay United, a club he had once guided to promotion, he probably thought that he would be given a fair chance to repeat his earlier success at Plainmoor. Instead, he was catapulted into the headlines as the football manager with the shortest appointment in the history of the game.

It was on 17 May 2007 that the former West Ham United and Fulham striker was introduced to a press conference to announce that he had replaced Keith Curle as head coach at Torquay. The press conference ended at 3.30pm and journalists were gathering up their belongings and heading for the exit when they were called back.

It was now 3.40pm. United, who had just finished bottom of the Football League, had been sold to a consortium. They had appointed Colin Lee as chief executive. Lee did not fancy Rosenior as the club's manager. Instead he had appointed Exeter City's assistant manager to the position, Paul Buckle.

Rosenior was philosophical: 'For it to happen ten minutes after I finished the press conference was a bit of a shock. But we had a good laugh about it afterwards. I wish them the very best of luck. They are going to sort me out a bit of compensation.'

'One of the craziest goals in history'
Liverpool beaten by a beach ball

When your luck is out, nothing seems to go your way. Ask the Liverpool supporters who were at Sunderland's Stadium of Light on 17 October 2009.

The Merseysiders were on their way to their lowest finishing position for years and, with it, the loss of a place in the following season's European Champions League.

What happened in that FA Premier League match at Sunderland just about summed up their year.

When Sunderland's Darren Bent shot for goal in the fifth minute, the Liverpool goalkeeper, Pepe Reina, appeared to have it covered. But then the football hit a beach ball. The match ball was deflected to Reina's right and into his net for the only goal of the game, with the beach ball just missing the post on his left. To add insult to injury, the beach ball, branded with the Liverpool crest, had been thrown on to the pitch by a Liverpool fan.

Pepe Reina

Reina wrote later: 'I have been asked so many times why I didn't just kick the beach ball off the pitch as soon as it was thrown on, but I only realised it was right in front of me when Andy Reid crossed the proper football into the box and there it was. Even after spotting it, I didn't think it was about to play a part in one of the craziest goals in English football history.'

A woman running the line?
Whatever next?

W hen Sky Sports commentators Andy Gray and Richard Keys made sexist remarks about female assistant referee Sian Massey – not to mention similar comments about Birmingham City's vice-chairman Karen Brady – before the Liverpool–Wolves FA Premier League match at Anfield in January 2011, they probably thought that their microphones were switched off. They weren't – and Gray and Keys ultimately paid with their jobs.

Keys was heard to say: 'Somebody better get down there and explain

Amy Fearn

offside to her.' Gray responded: 'Can you believe that? A female linesman. Women don't know the offside rule.'

Whoops! In fact female match officials had been contributing to football for quite some time already. Wendy Toms, from Dorset, was the first female to officiate as an assistant referee in the Football League back in 1994, and in the FA Premiership in 1997. It was just that Gray and Keys apparently hadn't noticed.

In fact, by the time the Sky duo agreed that a woman wasn't capable of running the line in a football match, a female had already refereed a Championship game. Amy Fearn was the fourth official when Coventry City met Nottingham Forest in a Championship match at the Ricoh Arena on 9 February

2010. With 20 minutes left to play, referee Tony Bates was forced to leave the field with a calf strain and Fearn, an economics graduate from Loughborough, took charge for the remainder of the match.

Unfortunately, Gray and Keys weren't the only unreconstructed misogynists when it came to football. In November 2006, Luton Town manager Mike Newell, angry with Fearn's decision not to award a penalty during Luton's 3-2 defeat by Queen's Park Rangers, had frothed at an after-match press conference: 'She shouldn't be here. I know that sounds sexist but I am sexist. This is not park football, so what are women doing here?'

Newell later apologised, saying: 'My apology to Amy Rayner [Fearn's maiden name], and to anyone I've offended, is unreserved. I was out of order and she has accepted it.' Newell was later fined a total of £6,500 and given a warning by his club.

Women officials became part of the senior game in the 1990s but they had been part of the lower levels of football for many years. In 1976, Pat Dunn of Weymouth became the first woman to referee an all-male match sanctioned by the FA when she took charge of an East Lulworth versus Freewheelers match in Dorset.

In October 1981, Elizabeth Forsdick became the first woman official in an FA Cup tie when she ran the line in the third qualifying tie between Burgess Hill Town and Carshalton Athletic. Nettie Honeyball would have been proud.

NOT TO BE SNIFFED AT

Of all the health problems that might severely restrict a footballer, an allergy to grass must be high on the list. Unfortunately for Yoan Gouffran of French Ligue 1 club Girondins de Bordeaux that is exactly what he suffers from. In October 2010 his manager, Jean Tigana, told the **Le Parisien** *newspaper: 'For a footballer, it's embarrassing.' In France's top division only two clubs, Nancy and Lorient, possessed synthetic pitches so Gouffran had to play 36 of 38 games that season on grass, and was ordered to seek medical help in managing his disorder.*

Cold comfort for Oldham supporters
Sub-zero wait for tickets rewarded only by heavy defeat

When League One club Oldham Athletic faced Liverpool in the FA Cup in January 2012, their fans probably anticipated a chilly Anfield reception from the Premier League club. But two Oldham supporters received a cold welcome of their own when they went to buy tickets from their club.

In the small hours of a winter's morning hundreds of fans queued, waiting for the Boundary Park ticket office to open. At 500ft (152m) above sea-level Oldham's home has the third highest elevation of any Football League ground. On this day it was also swept by driving rain and bitterly cold winds.

Oldham's manager, Paul Dickov, pitched in to distribute tea and coffee in an effort to keep supporters warm but the conditions proved too much for two fans who had to be treated for hypothermia. Both supporters eventually secured tickets – but was it all worth it? They were among 6,200 travelling fans who saw their team crash out to the tune of 5-1.

Incidentally, the Football League ground highest above sea level is West Bromwich Albion's The Hawthorns stadium at 551ft (168m) followed by Port Vale's Vale Park at 525ft (160m).

WHAT A DIFFERENCE 25 YEARS MAKE
When on 6 November 2011 Sir Alex Ferguson celebrated 25 years in charge of Manchester United, the top four clubs in the FA Premier League were Manchester City, Manchester United, Newcastle United and Chelsea. When Ferguson took over as United's manager on 6 November 1986 the bottom four teams in the old First Division were Newcastle United, Manchester City, Chelsea and Manchester United.

Handcuffed to a goalpost
Liverpool fan with an axe to grind

When John Foley emerged from the crowd at Goodison Park on 31 January 2012 and handcuffed himself to a goalpost, most fans thought that he was an Everton supporter protesting at the financial state of the club.

The clue, however, lay in the T-shirt that the 46-year-old was wearing. The protest message was directed at the budget airline, Ryanair, whose boss, Michael O'Leary, was apparently in the stands to watch the FA Premier League game between Everton and his favourite team, Manchester City. Mr Foley, a Liverpool FC supporter, said that he was protesting over his airline cabin attendant daughter being sacked by Ryanair.

Everton captain Phil Neville tried to convince Mr Foley to leave the pitch but police had to use bolt-cutters to remove the handcuffs and release him from the goal that City's Joe Hart was defending. Mr Foley was charged with going on to the playing area at a football match, and bailed to appear before Liverpool Magistrates Court. He apologised to both sets of supporters for holding up play for five minutes.

PICTURE CREDITS

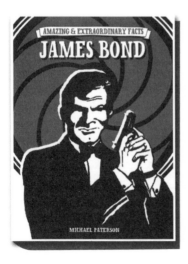

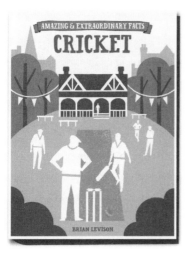

AMAZING & EXTRAORDINARY FACTS: CRICKET
Brian Levison
ISBN: 978-1-4463-0250-7

This essential companion for all cricket lovers documents the illustrious history of the gentleman's game. It is crammed full of fascinating feats, sticky wickets and intriguing trivia, so even if you don t like cricket, you'll love this. From the worst batsman in the world to the record innings that almost wasn't, this compelling collection of balls, bails, bats and blockholes is guaranteed to enthral.

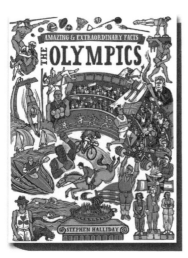

AMAZING & EXTRAORDINARY FACTS: THE OLYMPICS
Stephen Halliday
ISBN: 978-1-4463-0201-9

A unique and entertaining collection of facts surrounding the Olympic Games. From their origins in ancient Greece to the most famous Olympic medalists, the book covers a range of fascinating trivia for every sport lover to enjoy. You can discover the athletes who have set the marks for modern sporting excellence, and wonder at the records set by competitors across the years.